School Politics
in the Metropolis

Metropolitan America: Its Government and Politics Series

Under the Editorship of

Alan K. Campbell
*Dean of the Maxwell Graduate School
of Citizenship and Public Affairs*

School Politics
in the Metropolis

Philip J. Meranto
Assistant Professor
Institute of Government and Public Affairs
University of Illinois

Charles E. Merrill Publishing Company
A Bell & Howell Company
Columbus, Ohio

To my wife, Barbara

Standard Book Number 0-675-09340-6
Library of Congress Catalog Card Number: 75-113175

1 2 3 4 5 6 7 8 9 10–74 73 72 71 70

Printed in the United States of America

Preface

During the 1960's American urban school districts became engulfed in an unprecedented political conflict. By focusing on the impact of metropolitanization on suburban and city schools, this volume attempts to explain why such turmoil erupted. Much of the analysis emphasizes the failure of city school districts to meet the educational needs of its most recent and rapidly growing clientele—black students. This failure constitutes one of the major causes of current school controversies and promises to be the major issue confronting city schools in the decade ahead. The basic question is whether city school districts, aided by state and federal programs, can devise politically feasible strategies to provide quality education for black students.

I would like to thank several individuals who helped make this book possible. Dean Alan K. Campbell was instrumental in stimulating much of the thinking included in this volume and my interest in school politics. Samuel K. Gove, Director of the Institute of Government and Public Affairs, University of Illinois, and the Institute staff, particularly Margaret Jones and Loretta McKeighen, extended much assistance to me for which I am extremely grateful. Thanks is also extended to Dennis Judd, Joseph Pisciotte, David Ranney and David Tyack for reading an earlier draft of the manuscript and suggesting revisions. Finally, I am especially thankful to my wife, Barbara, for all the help and encouragement she provided while I was preparing this book.

Philip J. Meranto
Urbana, Illinois

Contents

List of Tables

American Education: Its Governmental Ideology and Characteristics

1

I. Introduction

Not many Americans would argue with the proposition that education occupies a prominent position in the institutional structure of American society. Since the founding of the nation, and increasingly so in recent times, Americans have expressed confidence in the notion that education is the means to many desirable ends. Substantial stress, for example, has been placed on the idea that education constitutes one of the cornerstones of a democratic society because it enhances the citizens' ability to make intelligent public policy decisions. Without a well-educated and informed public, the proper functioning of democracy is supposedly threatened.

Education has also been viewed by many groups in the society as a primary avenue to economic and social mobility. It is often asserted that education is the vital key to the American opportunity structure; consequently, youngsters are encouraged to absorb more schooling than their parents did. The decrease of unskilled and semi-skilled jobs and the transformation of America into a highly technical, "credential conscious" society adds considerable urgency to this latter pronouncement.

The socialization function of education has also been expanded, both qualitatively and quantitively, in contemporary times. Historically, schools supplemented the work of the family and the church in socializing the younger generation. Presently, however, it is becoming more common for the school to act as a substitute for the family and church. Individuals now start school at a younger age, stay longer, and are exposed to a wider variety of socializing experiences within the school context than ever before. Additionally, more and longer educational experiences for as many Americans as possible has become the popular formula for solving a wide range of social problems. Juvenile delinquency, unemployment and racial strife are but a few social problems which supposedly would be mastered if every American received all the education he was capable of absorbing.

Concrete testimony to this manifold faith in education is illustrated by the fact that Americans spend more on education than they do on any other domestic governmental service ($60 billion in 1968-69) and that, at last count, some 58 million Americans were enrolled in the nation's schools and colleges.[1]

II. Scholars and School Governance

Given the social importance ascribed to the education function and the enormous amount of resources which are poured into this governmental service, it is surprising that scholars who specialize in government have, until very recently, paid so little attention to the governance of education. Although numerous studies of local community decision-making have been conducted since Floyd Hunter published his famous study of Atlanta, Georgia in 1953, few of these studies have focused on such questions as: "who makes and influences decisions concerning school policy and what is the impact of school policy on various citizens?"[2]

To some extent, the general neglect of such questions may result from the frame of reference utilized by many of the scholars who conducted the early studies in community power structures, and from

---

[1] National Education Association, *Financial Status of the Public Schools, 1969* (Washington, D.C.: NEA, 1969), p. 5.

[2] Floyd Hunter, *Community Power Structure* (New York: Doubleday and Co., 1953). Some recent volumes which do focus on such questions are: David Rogers, *110 Livingston Street* (New York: Random House, 1968); Marilyn Gittell and T. Edward Hollander, *Six Urban School Districts: A Comparative Study of Institutional Response* (New York: Frederick A. Praeger, Publishers, 1968); Marilyn Gittell, *Participants and Participation: A Study of School Policy in New York City* (New York: Center for Urban Education, 1967).

the ideological myths which educators have built around school governance.

Concerning the first point, many scholars relied on what is commonly referred to as the stratification theory of community power. This frame of reference posits that the pattern of social stratification in a community is the primary determinant of the pattern of governmental decision-making.[3] The basic notions are that a single power elite, consisting of upper class individuals, rules local community life; that political and civic leaders are subordinate to the power elite; and that the upper-class power elite rules in its own interests, which generally conflict with the interests of lower classes. This image of power distribution in the local community suggests that a small group of economic elites determines policy in significant areas of community affairs, including education. Hunter, for example, writes:

> Most institutions and associations are subordinate to the interests of the policy-makers who operate in the economic sphere of community life in Regional City [Atlanta]. The institutions of the family, church, state, education, and the like draw sustenance from economic institutional sources and are thereby subordinate to this particular institution more than any other. . . . We see both the institutions and the formal associations playing a vital role in the execution of determined policy, but the formulation of policy often takes place outside these formalized groupings.[4]

It is possible that acceptance of this conception of community decision-making discouraged the in-depth analysis of policy-making within specific functional areas. Why should researchers spend a lot of time investigating how schoolmen, board members, and citizens work out educational policy if they suspected that a small group of wealthy men were huddled in the country club formulating not only educational policy, but policies for a wide variety of community issues?

Fortunately, this view of local community policy-making was challenged by several scholars who conducted studies of the governmental decision process in such cities as New York, New Haven, Chicago and

---

[3] An analysis of this approach is presented in Nelson W. Polsby, *Community Power and Political Theory* (New Haven: Yale University Press, 1963). For some recent statements on the continuing debate of this topic see: Jack L. Walker, "A Critique of the Elitist Theory of Democracy," *American Political Science Review* (June, 1966), pp. 286-295, and Richard M. Merelman, "On the Neo-Elitist Critique of Community Power," *American Political Science Review* (June, 1968), pp. 451-460.

[4] Hunter, *op. cit.*, pp. 81-82.

Syracuse.[5] Although each of these studies was conducted in a somewhat different manner, all of the researchers arrived at a similar
conclusion—a conclusion quite different from the elitest findings of
Hunter and others. They found that, although a relatively small proportion of the total population in any city was actually involved in the
formulation of policy and decision-making, there was not a single
group which dominated in all functional areas. Instead, they discovered a pattern of specialization in policy-making along functional
lines. Each decisional area, such as urban renewal, transportation,
health, welfare, and education, tended to contain a group of individuals
who were highly influential in policy-making for that particular function; only a few individuals were also involved in other decisional
areas. In contrast to the single, economic elite profile, the scholars
suggested a power pattern generally referred to as nonoverlapping,
multiple elites. This finding implied that the power structure in many
large cities was polylithic rather than monolithic, and that the former
distribution of power constituted an acceptable (in terms of traditionally democratic theory) participatory system that allowed a variety of individuals to become involved in the decision-making process.

One might argue, however, that the pattern of policy-making by
functional specialization says nothing about the relative participatory
possibilities *within* particular functional areas. Indeed, the material
which follows illustrates that the education function in the urban
North has been a relatively closed decisional system, and that this
characteristic has important implications for the intensive controversies
which currently surround American school politics. In recent years
scholars have begun to recognize this linkage and are devoting greater
attention to it.

III. School Government and the Doctrines of Separatism, No-Politics, Professionalism, and No-Conflict

Another factor which may have contributed to the unusual lack of
scholarly interest in school policy-making relates to the ideology sur-

---

[5] Wallace S. Sayre and Herbert Kaufman, *Governing New York City* (New
York: Russell Sage Foundation, 1960); Robert A. Dahl, *Who Governs?* (New
Haven: Yale University Press, 1961); Edward Banfield, *Political Influence*
(New York: The Free Press, 1961); Roscoe C. Martin and Frank J. Munger, *et al.*,
Decisions in Syracuse (Bloomington: Indiana University Press, 1961); Linton C.
Freeman, *Patterns of Local Community Leadership* (Indianapolis: Bobbs-Merrill
Co., 1968).

rounding school governance. Educators have been notably successful in developing and selling to others a set of ideological doctrines which have given them considerable autonomy of operation and insulation from public inspection. One of these doctrines is often referred to as the principle of localism. Professional educators, along with many state legislators and school board members, have expounded the view, which has been accepted by the general public, that education is primarily a local responsibility. It has been strongly argued that the establishment of educational policy and the control of school activities should rest in the hands of local officials. Local autonomy is deemed necessary because every community has different population characteristics, educational needs, and resources.

Another of the educators' beliefs, which is to some extent an extension of the localism principle, is that education is a unique governmental service which must be separated from other local governments. In other words, not only should educational policy be controlled at the local level of government; but within the local community, schools should be protected from control or influence by other governmental officials. This quest for local independence emanates from several beliefs held by schoolmen, the most basic being that since education is such an important function, it must be "kept out of politics." This fear of political involvement grows out of the effort to isolate the education of children from the "corrupt political machines" which controlled many local and state governments, including school systems, during the late nineteenth and early twentieth centuries. It is also related to the recognition on the part of educators that in a governmental system where the fortunes of political parties wax and wane, it would be detrimental for the schools to become too closely associated with a particular political party. Additionally, educators have apparently decided that if they are to be accepted as professionals in a society which stresses objective expertise, they must project the image that their activities are above partisan politics. And finally, schoolmen have argued for independent status on budgetary grounds. Although much conflicting evidence exists concerning the impact of fiscal independence on schools, many educators, in opposition to economists and political scientists, take the position that schools are able to gain greater fiscal support when their budgets are separated from the general municipal budget. They also feel that only professional educators are qualified to determine how much money is needed and how it should be allocated to provide the community with an adequate school system. Since the professionals lack primary control over these matters in a dependent school system, school officials argue vigorously for independence as the only way to protect the schools from the meddling of municipal officials who must make budgetary decisions within a "political context."[6]

That educators have been successful, in a structural sense, in their quest for independence is illustrated by the fact that about 95 per cent of the school districts in the nation are independent districts. That is, they exist as separate governmental jurisdictions divorced from the other local governments which occupy the same geographic area. In a thought-provoking article written in 1959, Thomas Eliot convincingly argued that this separation and the ideological doctrines of school government did not and should not place education outside the purview of political analysis. He argued that the schools were thoroughly involved in the political process and that political analysts had a professional obligation to study school politics.[7]

Eliot and others have rightly pointed out that while school districts are ordinarily separated from other local political units, it is important to note that they are similar to the other governments in several respects. Like all local governments, school districts are established by state action and, despite the doctrine of localism, the ultimate authority over school districts rests with the state government. School districts also have fixed territorial boundaries, legal constituencies, legislative bodies which are directly or indirectly responsible to the electorate, administrative officers and bureaucracies. They possess the authority to levy taxes and allocate public resources. And although their service is limited to a single public service, school districts are expected to perform this service within the context of our traditional democratic political culture by serving the people, providing for citizen participation, and responding to citizen needs.

While education is fundamentally a state function, the state has delegated much of the responsibility for governing the schools to local officials. Consequently, the citizens of the local community generally elect members to the board of education, which then operates as the

---

[6] Educational ideology as it relates to politics is discussed in: Thomas H. Eliot, "Toward an Understanding of Public School Politics," *American Political Science Review* (December, 1959), pp. 1032-1051, and Roscoe C. Martin, *Government and the Suburban School* (Syracuse: Syracuse University Press, 1962). A summary of the pros and cons concerning independence can be found in Seymour Sacks and David C. Ranney, *The Allocation of Fiscal Resources to Large City Schools* (Syracuse University Press, forthcoming). Also see: Robert H. Salisbury, "Schools and Politics in the Big City," *Harvard Educational Review* (Summer, 1967), pp. 408-425, and David W. Minar, "Community Politics and School Boards," *School Board Journal* (March, 1967), pp. 33-39.

[7] Eliot, *op. cit.*

legal decision-making body for the school district.[8] The board assumes the responsibility for formulating major school policy, developing programs, employing personnel, levying taxes, providing educationally related services, and managing the physical facilities of the district.[9]

Perhaps the key decision made by the board is the selection of a professional administrator, the superintendent of schools. Drawing from his professional training, the superintendent submits policy recommendations to the board for their consideration and assumes responsibility for implementing policies determined by the board, although the line between policy-making and administration of policy is usually blurred.

Considering the importance of education and the legal power of the school board over education policy, there is a surprising lack of systematic studies concerning the nomination practices and election of board members. The most comprehensive study of school districts indicates that 44 per cent of the school board candidates are nominated by petitions, 22 per cent by individual announcements, 8 per cent by primary elections, 3 per cent by caucuses, 1 per cent by school meeting conventions, and 20 per cent by some combination of these methods.[10] Although popular petition and individual announcements are the prevailing methods of nomination, the few studies which do deal with this topic suggest that access to a school board slate is rather carefully controlled in some communities.[11] Goldhammer, for instance, states that an informal screening process operates in many school districts to insure that candidates exemplify "certain values . . . and certain characteristics which influential people in the community hold to be important for the maintenance of community stability."[12] He makes the additional point that incumbent school board members, by virtue of their knowledge of laws related to nomination procedures, of coming elections, and their contacts with key groups, exert considerable

---

[8] Although some school boards are appointed, the overwhelming proportion, about 85 per cent, are elected by popular vote. See Alphenus L. White, *Local School Boards: Organization and Practices* (Washington, D.C.: U.S. Office of Education, 1962), p. 10.

[9] Keith Goldhammer, *The School Board* (New York: The Center for Applied Research in Education, Inc., 1964); Edward Tuttle, *School Board Leadership in America* (Danville, Illinois: Interstate Printers and Publishers, 1958).

[10] White, *op. cit.*, p. 10.

[11] See, for example, National Commision for the Defense of Democracy Through Education, *Indianapolis, Indiana: A Study of the Sudden Forced Resignation of a Superintendent* (Washington, D.C.: National Education Association, 1960), and Martin, *op. cit.*, pp. 45-46.

[12] *The School Board*, p. 27.

influence over the nomination process. During periods of stable school-community relations, the school board may be virtually a self-perpetu-ating group.

David Minar, in his analysis of 48 suburban school districts in the Chicago metropolitan area, found that approximately half utilized the caucus method to select school board members.[13] He reported that in so-called "high status-low conflict" districts, the caucus method monop-olized board nominations, while in the "lower status-high conflict" districts, access to nominations was essentially open. In the high-status districts (based on the socio-economic characteristics of residents), the caucuses were fostered by Parent-Teacher Associations, League of Women Voters, and other local organizations to select "acceptable" candidates by interviewing prospective nominees and consulting with the presiding board members and the administration. Two key features of the caucus system, as practiced in these districts, are that "the job seeks the man, not the man the job" and caucus nominees are not opposed by "outside" candidates. Emphasis is placed on utilizing the caucus as a means of restricting conflict or potential conflict before it can become a public issue so that the school board and superintendent may keep the system operating smoothly. Minar concludes that:

> The use of the caucus is thus one aspect of the general thrust toward conflict suppression; it also reflects the notion that education is a sacred cow, and particularly a sacred cow best nurtured by experts in its care and feeding.[14]

The desire to shield the schools from the ordinary political atmos-phere also shows up in the practice of holding school board elections separately from other local elections. This procedure allows schoolmen to emphasize the independence of school government from the con-troversial issues and candidates involved in municipal government. One of the latent outcomes of this practice is small voter turnout in many school elections. Indeed, Minar's study found that, on the aver-age, only 9 per cent of the eligible voters showed up at the polls be-tween 1958 and 1962 in the 48 suburban school districts he studied.[15] From the perspective of democratic theory, this low level of citizen

---

13 *Educational Decision-making in Suburban Communities* (Washington D.C.: U.S. Office of Education, Cooperative Research No. 2440, 1966) and "The Com-munity Basis of Conflict in School System Politics," *American Sociological Review* (December, 1966), pp. 822-835.

14 *American Sociological Review*, p. 830.

15 *Ibid.*, p. 824.

participation may suggest an unhealthy situation. Some educators, however, have chosen to interpret this nonparticipation as symbolic of public satisfaction with the manner in which the schools are handled.[16] The little empirical evidence which does exist on this question suggests that the point may be valid in certain communities, since voter participation is generally higher in those districts where the schools are entangled in conflict.[17]

Another characteristic of school board elections, and a logical extension of the apolitical nature of educational ideology and the practices discussed thus far, is the widespread custom of school board candidates' running on a nonpartisan basis. The attitude expressed in this instance is that if there is no Republican or Democratic way to build a road, there certainly is no partisan way to run a school system. Nonpartisanship as it relates to party labels, of course, does not mean that partisan issues are absent from school governance. In fact, there are countless examples of bitter partisan school conflicts (as will be illustrated later) but to a large extent the controversies are managed outside the framework of the two major political parties.

Perhaps the most significant outcome of these nomination and election procedures is the social composition of school boards. Several studies have revealed that men with above-average formal education who are in business, managerial and professional occupations are highly over-represented on school boards.[18] These findings inevitably raise the question of the extent to which the social composition of school boards results in biased social, economic, and political perspectives. More specifically, the query has been posed as to whether board members represent a "conservative" point of view which is consequently endorsed as the accepted system of values in the schools, but which is compatible with only a selected segment of the community. Some investigations which have dealt with this subject conclude that most school board members do hold views which are more conservative

---

[16] Roscoe C. Martin, *Government and the Suburban School* (Syracuse: Syracuse University Press, 1962), pp. 46-47.

[17] Minar found that "districts high in participation are likely to be high in dissent," with dissent referring to the proportion of all votes cast which were cast for losing candidates (*American Sociological Review*, p. 824).

[18] The classic study in this field is George S. Counts, *The Social Composition of Boards of Educations* (Chicago: The University of Chicago Press, 1927). For a summary of more recent studies see Goldhammer, *op. cit.,* pp. 89-94. On suburban districts in particular, consult Martin, *op. cit.* and Minar, *op. cit.* Martin concluded from his sample that "It is clear that the typical suburban school board represents the economically and socially advantaged of the community" (p. 51).

than those of the general population.[19] On the other hand, it has also been suggested that, while board members may possess "conservative" views on broad social issues, there is some evidence to indicate that they are "liberal," i.e., willing to experiment with new ideas and changes on educational matters such as curriculum development.[20] This latter point, however, overlooks the question of school board influence on the *content* of the new curriculum. In sum, more research is needed on the relationship between the social and political attitudes of school board members and the set of values endorsed, either consciously or unconsciously, by the school system. This is particularly the case for large urban districts, where the representation of minority groups on school boards lags far behind the minority group proportion of the school population.

The attitudes of school board members perhaps have their most important impact on school matters through the board's selection or retention of a superintendent of schools, since the superintendent is in many respects the key individual in the school's decision-making process. The board retains the legal authority to make final policy decisions, but it is accepted procedure for the superintendent to recommend the preferred policy alternative. According to the norms of professional educators:

> . . . the board must rely for leadership on its chief executive officer, the superintendent. He should recommend a course of action for the board except when he himself cannot decide on a course of action. It is then up to the board to accept, reject, or accept with modifications the superintendent's recommendation. In case of rejection, preferred practice is for the board to refer the subject under consideration to the superintendent for further study and a new recommendation.[21]

The profession's justification for centralizing the policy recommendation function in the hands of the superintendent is that he alone possesses the required expertise to best understand the feasible policy alternatives and their likely educational impact on the school system. This expertise supposedly results from the superintendent's profes-

[19] Keith Goldhammer, "Community Power Structure and School Board Membership," *American School Board Journal* (March, 1955), pp. 23-25; Leonard Garmire, "A Study of the Attitudes of School Board Members as They Relate to the Reasons for Seeking Office," *Oregon School Study Council Bulletin*, Vol. 6, No. 2 (Eugene, Oregon: School of Education, University of Oregon, 1962).

[20] Robert J. Havighurst and Bernice I. Neugarten, *Society and Education* (2nd ed.; Boston: Allyn and Bacon, Inc., 1962).

[21] American Association of School Administrators, *School Board Superintendent Relationships* (Washington, D.C.: The Association, 1956), p. 36.

sional training and experience, which provide him with knowledge
about school matters unmatched by the lay school board members and
ordinary citizens. In addition to his expert knowledge, the superintendent's authority is reinforced by his professional status in a society
where professionalism is valued; he devotes his full working time to
school business, whereas board members can only devote part-time
attention; he generally is in office longer than most board members;
he has a staff at his disposal which can aid his performance in numerous ways (particularly in controlling information); and finally, as head
of the bureaucratic structure, he can speak for the entire administration, whereas the board may be divided on particular issues.[22]

Despite these impressive sources of authority, superintendents and
school boards in scores of communities have clashes over their respective spheres of decision-making. The theoretical proposition that the
board makes policy based upon recommendations from the superintendent, and that he in turn administers the policy, is seldom true in
practice. Gross, for example, in his study of school districts in New
England, found that superintendents view board members as a major
obstacle in their efforts to execute their jobs in what they consider a
professional manner.[23] Conversely, other studies have found that some
board members feel that the superintendent has usurped the authority
of the board.

Whether a conflict exists over the relative spheres of the superintendent and the board, disagreement over a particular school policy,
or whatever, the fact that a school conflict becomes public is most
unfortunate from the educators' perspective. Schoolmen, after all, have
taken every precaution to see to it that the schools function without
becoming involved in public controversy, and to the extent that such
controversy occurs, they have failed. Consequently, their ability to
run the schools in an insulated fashion is threatened. Conflict not only
supposedly disrupts the serenity of the educational process, but, from
a seldom-mentioned pragmatic view, it may weaken the public's confidence in the schools, thus endangering financial support.[24] Since

---

[22] For detailed treatments of this topic see Minar, *Educational, Decision-making
in Suburban Communities*, pp. 92-96; John F. Gallagher, *Decision-making in Public
Education: Views from the Professional Literature* (University of California, Davis:
Institute of Government and Public Affairs, 1965), pp. 17-21. Alan Rosenthal,
"Community Leadership and Public School Politics: Two Case Studies" (Princeton
University, Unpublished Ph.D. dissertation, 1960) and Joseph Pois, *The School
Board Crisis: A Chicago Case Study* (Chicago: Educational Methods, Inc., 1964).
[23] Neal Gross, *Who Runs Our Schools?* (New York: John Wiley and Sons, Inc.,
1958), p. 36.
[24] On this point see Eliot, *op. cit.*, pp. 1041-1042.

virtually every school district must at some time or another seek public approval of a bond issue or referendum, educators are understandably anxious to present an image of consensus rather than disagreement on the expert operation of the schools. Additionally, any significant amount of controversy tends to undermine the claim of professional expertise on the part of school administrators and teachers. For these reasons, then, professional educators have attempted to conduct school business in a non-conflict atmosphere.

IV. The Insulation of Public Education

The ideological doctrines and governmental features of the education function obviously influence the character of educational decision-making in any particular school district. However, the potential participants in the policy-making process of these separate governments are essentially the same in all school systems. The so-called core of the decisional system (where formal authority is concentrated) is occupied, as noted earlier, by the local board of education and the superintendent. Very close to the core is the school bureaucracy, including central administrators, supervisory staff, field administrators, and organizations representing each of these groups. Further from the center are teachers and their organizations and parents and their organizations. Other potential participants are educational interest groups (both *ad hoc* and permanent), noneducational interest groups, and other public officials.

It has been suggested that the participation of these potential actors in school policy-making can generally take three forms: (1) *closed—* only the core actors, the board members, the superintendent and his close associates, participate; (2) *limited—*middle range supervisors, teachers and specialized educational interest groups participate; (3) *wide—*various interest groups such as civil rights groups, neighborhood organizations, parent groups, other public officials and so forth, participate in a meaningful manner.[25]

The few empirical studies on participation patterns in school policy-making indicate that many urban city school systems have generally been *closed* systems. In his study of New Haven, Dahl concluded that: "direct influence over decisions in public education seems to be exerted

---

[25] For a variation of these groupings, see Marilyn Gittell, *Participants and Participation: A Study of School Policy in New York City* (New York: Center for Urban Education, 1967), p. 4.

almost entirely by public officials."[26] He identified these public officials as the board members, the superintendent of schools, and the mayor of New Haven, who, although he appointed board members, subscribed to the local norms that the schools be insulated from partisan politics.

A more extensive study, which included the school system in Baltimore, Chicago, Detroit, New York, Philadelphia and St. Louis, contains a similar finding. The authors concluded that:

> . . . public education . . . has over the years become perhaps the most nonpublic of governmental services. Public school systems have removed decision-making from the agents closest to the school child— the teachers and parents. . . . The concept of public accountability has been abandoned. The school professionals have convinced the various public interests that only they are qualified to make policy. Whether a district is fiscally independent or dependent does not influence the fact that a small core of school people control decisions for public education in every large city. . . . The insulation of public education is two-fold: bureaucratic centralization (or more accurately overcentralization) which is a product of size, reinforced by an ideological rationale of professionalism, which is a product of the vested interests of the educationalists. The result is a static, internalized, isolated system which has been unable to respond to vastly changing needs and demands of large city populations.[27]

A parallel judgment was reached at the conclusion of a five-year study of the New York City School District, in which the researcher portrayed the system as the epitome of overcentralization of decision-making and bureaucratic pathology.[28] Writings on the Boston and Washington, D.C. schools suggest similar patterns in those cities.[29]

The ideological creeds of educators and the resulting insulation of public schools have come under heavy fire from segments of the public during the last decade or so. Schoolmen have found it increasingly difficult to operate the schools in the traditional fashion, and have found that the schools are often at the very center of the most heated

---

[26] Dahl, *Who Governs?* p. 151.

[27] Marilyn Gittell and T. Edward Hollander, *Six Urban School Districts: A Comparative Study of Institutional Response* (New York: Frederick A. Praeger, Publishers, 1968), pp. 196-197.

[28] Rogers, *op. cit.*

[29] Peter Schrag, *Village School Downtown* (Boston: Beacon Press, 1967); Jonathan Kozol, *Death at an Early Age* (New York: Bantam Books, 1967); and A. Harry Passow, *Summary of a Report on the Washington, D.C. Public Schools* (New York: Teachers College, Columbia University, 1967).

and intense local political controversies.[30] This volume demonstrates why this situation has evolved. It will be shown that education, like other governmental services in contemporary America, is performing in a society which is undergoing rapid change that has forced all levels and units of government to reexamine their roles in various public service areas. Governmental arrangements, ideological dogmas, and patterns of policy-making which may have been appropriate in the past are quite often obsolete today, and will no doubt be more so in the future.

Many agents of change, of course, have contributed to this situation. However, one of the major agents of societal change in post-World War II America is the process of metropolitanization. This process, which is fully discussed in the following chapter, has generated a social, economic, fiscal and political environment which, on the one hand, has made it virtually impossible to shield the education function from conflict, and on the other hand, has stimulated a rethinking of the appropriate relationship of the state and federal governments to local school districts. In other words, the fact that America has become a metropolitan society carries important implications for the governance of education. Consequently, a major portion of this volume examines the impact of metropolitanism on schools in the urban North. Emphasis will be placed on: (1) how the metropolitan process has influenced the environment in which urban school districts function; (2) the major political problems which have arisen from this new environment; (3) the manner in which these political problems have altered the traditional governance of schools; (4) the quest for new intergovernmental educational arrangements; and (5) the future of urban education.

---

[30] During the 1968-1969 school year, the New York schools became entangled in a decentralization controversy which stimulated intense conflict throughout the city over educational and noneducational issues.

The Metropolitan Process and Educational Implications

2

I. Urbanization: The Metropolitan Forerunner

To understand how metropolitanization has contributed to altering the environment of schools, it is necessary to define the concept clearly. This definition is particularly important in relation to the concept of urbanization, since it is not unusual to find these two terms employed synonymously with no attempt to indicate that they refer to related but different processes and conditions. In this respect, perhaps the most fundamental distinction is that it was necessary for America to become an urban nation before it could became a metropolitan nation; that the process of urbanization is a prerequisite to metropolitanization. The difference between these two processes and their concomitant conditions becomes evident if we examine and contrast their basic characteristics.

Although the United States has contained an important strain of urbanism since its very founding (the American Revolution was plotted in cities), it was not until the latter part of the nineteenth century that the trend of urbanization began to emerge as the dominant feature

15

of the nation.[1] Particularly in the years after the Civil War and
during the first half of the twentieth century (with the exception of the
depression decade), a rapidly increasing proportion of Americans
resided and made their livelihood in the growing cities. Throughout
this period American underwent a transformation from an essentially
rural, agriculturally-oriented society to an urban, manufacturing and
commercially-based society. This transformation resulted from a variety
of factors which collectively have been termed urbanization—the
process whereby population and non-farm economic activities become
concentrated in relatively large, densely compacted centers called
cities.

One of the basic factors contributing to American urbanization has
been termed "rural push," referring to the fact that during this period
American farmers continued to improve their capacity to increase
production per acre and per man through advanced agricultural practices. As a consequence of these improvements, a surplus food and
labor supply developed in the countryside. The food and labor surplus
had the double effect of permitting more numerous and larger sized
cities to exist because of the available food supply and by creating the
urban manpower pool which had resulted from workers being pushed
from the farmlands.

The other basic factor underpinning urbanization is often referred
to as "urban pull." Technological changes not only had an impact on
the countryside, but influenced the potentialities of the growing cities
as well. The harnessing of steam as a source of energy, on the one hand,
increased the possibilities of mass production by machinery and, on
the other hand, made it feasible for railroads to multiply and extend
into the hinterland where raw materials could be loaded and shipped
to the cities for processing and marketing. Both of these developments
stimulated the creation of a wide variety of jobs which absorbed the
workers pushed off the farms and attracted additional workers from
the American hinterland and Europe as well. In fact, a large proportion of the approximately 35 million immigrants who arrived in America during the nineteenth and twentieth centuries settled in the cities,
where they contributed to the population growth and mixture. The
city acted as a magnet in both economic and social terms. Characterized by outstanding schools, churches, newspapers, libraries, book-

---

[1] The most thorough discussion concerning the role of urbanism in early American history is contained in two volumes by Carl Bridenbaugh, *Cities in the
Wilderness* (New York: Capricorn Books Edition, 1964) and *Cities in Revolt*
(New York: Capricorn Books Edition, 1964). Early nineteenth-century urbanism
is also thoughtfully examined in Richard Wade, *The Urban Frontier* (Chicago:
The University of Chicago Press, 1959) and Constance Green, *American Cities
in the Growth of the Nation* (London: John De Graff, 1957).

stores, art galleries, museums, theaters, amusement parks and opera houses, the cities were particularly attractive to young adults in rural areas who were anxious to pursue a more varied life than the countryside provided. The combination of economic and social opportunities proved irresistible to many, and the path from the countryside to urban centers became well-worn.[2]

This concentration of people with various backgrounds, non-farm economic activities, and social institutions in relatively large, densely populated communities constitute the basic features of urbanization and characterize the development of American society during much of the twentieth century. Before World War II, this trend was interrupted only during the depression decade, when the growth of cities came to a virtual standstill and several large cities actually declined in population. However, the war economy revitalized the nation and the cities; once again a stream of newcomers, particularly Negroes from the rural South, migrated to urban centers.[3]

In summary, during the period following the Civil War through the end of World War II, American cities, particularly those in the Northeast and Midwest, experienced tremendous population growth, rapid economic development, and considerable fiscal strength. Additionally, the cities housed the wealthier and more highly educated segments of the population, who were attracted by the economic, cultural, and educational opportunities. It is true that the cities also experienced many problems during this period, but the problems were related to growth, not decline.

II. Metropolitanization: The Shift from Centralization to Decentralization

In the years following the end of World War II, however, the major population and economic trends associated with urbanization underwent a significant alteration. The *dominant* flow of people, jobs, and

---

[2] The general characteristics of post-Civil War urbanization in America are discussed in Arthur M. Schlesinger, *The Rise of the City 1878-1898* (New York: The Macmillan Company, 1933); Adna F. Weber, *The Growth of Cities in the Nineteenth Century* (New York: The Macmillan Company, 1899); and Blake McKelvey, *The Urbanization of America, 1860-1915* (New Brunswick: Rutgers University Press, 1963). One should also consult the volume edited by Philip Hauser and Leo Schmore, *The Study of Urbanization* (New York: John Wiley & Sons, Inc., 1965) and Constance Green, *The Rise of Urban America* (New York: Harper & Row, Publishers, 1965).

[3] The restrictive immigration laws passed during the 1920's drastically reduced the number of immigrants moving into American cities after that decade, so that the recent urban newcomers are predominately native rural dwellers with a strain of Puerto Ricans and Mexicans. See Oscar Handlin, *The Newcomers* (Garden City, New York: Doubleday and Company, Inc., 1959).

economic activities no longer gravitated toward cities, but shifted from cities to the surrounding suburban communities. This process and its various social, economic and political concomitants have been designated as metropolitanization. In contrast to the term urbanization, which denotes the centralization of people and activities, the metropolitan concept stresses the spill-over or decentralization of urban population and activities beyond the governmental boundaries of core cities into the surrounding areas. It would be inaccurate to suggest that metropolitanization is an entirely recent development, since it began at a noticeable pace in the latter part of the nineteenth century; however, its predominance has characterized the post-war period, as is shown by the data presented in Table 1.

TABLE 1

Population Distribution and Growth in Central Cities
and Outside Central Cities: 1900-1965
(Conterminous United States)

	Central Cities		Outside Central City	
	Per cent of Metropolitan Population	Per cent Increase	Per cent of Metropolitan Population	Per cent Increase
1900	62.1	—	37.9	—
1910	64.6	37.1	35.4	23.6
1920	66.0	27.7	34.0	20.0
1930	64.6	24.3	35.4	32.3
1940	62.7	5.6	37.3	14.6
1950	58.6	14.7	41.4	35.9
1960	51.4	10.7	48.6	48.5
1965	48.1	3.2	51.9	17.7

Source: U.S. Bureau of the Census, *U.S. Census of Population: 1960 Selected Area Reports, Standard Metropolitan Statistical Areas* and *Current Population Reports,* Series P-20, No. 151, April 19, 1966.

The statistics included in this table summarize three relevant population trends: (1) the distribution of population within metropolitan areas[4] remained approximately the same between 1900 and 1940,

---

[4] The Census Bureau definition of the metropolitan area, including the central city and suburban ring, is followed throughout this book. That definition is as follows: "Except in New England, a standard metropolitan statistical area (an SMSA) is a county or group of contiguous counties which contain at least one city of 50,000 inhabitants or more or 'twin cities' with a combined population of at least 50,000. In addition to the county, or counties, containing such a city or cities, contiguous counties are included in an SMSA if, according to certain criteria, they are essentially metropolitan in character and are socially and economically integrated with the central city." In New England, towns are used instead of counties.

with 62 per cent of the inhabitants living in the central cities and about 38 per cent living outside the central cities; (2) from 1940 to the present, this distribution has steadily shifted, so that by 1965 a majority of the metropolitan population (52 per cent) resided outside the cities and 48 per cent lived within the core cities; and (3) the suburban population is currently not only a majority, but has been growing since 1940 at a rate of almost four times the growth of central cities.

This decline in the proportion of the metropolitan population living in central cities represents for many cities, particularly those in the largest metropolitan areas, an absolute decline in the core city population. Table 2 illustrates this decline, showing the per cent of population change for both central city and outside central city between 1950 and 1960 for selected large metropolitan areas. The few instances of an increase in central city population were caused, in most cases, by

TABLE 2

Population Change in 15 Largest SMSAs
Central City and Outside Central City: 1950-1960

	Central City		Outside Central City	
	1960 (000)	Per cent Change Since 1950	1960 (000)	Per cent Change Since 1950
New York	7,781	− 1.4	2,912	75.0
Chicago	3,550	− 1.9	2,670	71.5
Los Angeles[a]	2,823	27.1	3,919	82.6
Philadelphia	2,002	− 3.3	2,340	46.3
Detroit	1,670	− 9.7	2,092	79.3
Baltimore	939	− 1.1	787	72.4
Houston	938	57.4	304	44.8
Cleveland	876	− 4.2	920	67.2
Washington	763	− 4.8	661	87.0
St. Louis	750	−12.5	1,310	51.9
Milwaukee	741	16.3	452	41.7
San Francisco[b]	1,159	− 4.5	1,075	55.0
Boston	697	−13.0	1,892	17.6
Dallas	679	56.4	403	30.7
New Orleans	627	10.0	240	109.6
United States (All SMSAs)	58,004	10.7	54,880	48.6

[a] Includes Long Beach
[b] Includes Oakland
Source: U.S. Bureau of the Census, *U.S. Census of Populations: 1960* Vol. 1, Characteristics of the Population, part A. Number of Inhabitants, Table 33.

annexation rather than by population growth within the original boundaries of the central city. In sum, it is quite clear that the population within the largest metropolitan areas has been decentralizing at a rapid pace.

Several interrelated developments have stimulated this trend toward suburbanization. One cluster of factors consists of attitudes and values held by segments of the population concerning the desirability of city living versus suburban living. Public opinion surveys conducted among former city dwellers consistently show that the move to suburbia has generally been motivated by wishes to flee the congestion, noise, and dirtiness of the city for a more spacious, serene and "better" environment for children. Basically, the responses represent a desire on the part of families, particularly those with young children, for a detached house on a substantial plot of land in a community which stresses "family living" and has a sound, if not excellent, school system. Scholars who attempt to probe beneath these responses find that ethnic considerations, i.e., "We wanted to get away from the Negroes," while not often initially verbalized, are important. Indeed, the growing number of racial conflicts which have occurred in many American cities since the summer of 1964 has undoubtedly increased the importance of this latter variable. Other writers suggest that the exodus to suburbia is based on the yearning to escape the corrupt, machine-controlled politics of the city for what Robert Wood has termed "miniature republics" —small communities where personal involvement, participation, and control over nonpartisan government is possible.

Economic and technological developments contributed to the ability of individuals to fulfill these desires. Fundamentally, the income available to large segments of the population during the post-World War II years increased to the point where the financial means to live in suburbia and work in the city was no longer limited to the select well-to-do. More and more individuals found that their economic status made it possible (although in some cases with considerable strain) for them to afford commuting costs. Also, the increased availability of low down-payment, low interest rate, long-term mortgages guaranteed by the Federal government under its Federal Housing Agency programs substantially increased the number of families who could purchase new detached housing in the suburbs.

The prevalent use of the automobile also played a crucial role in the suburbanization process. Although the use of the automobile began to be widespread in the 1920's, the economic depression of the 1930's and the war needs of the 1940's postponed the real impact of automobile travel as the primary means of transportation until the years following

World War II. Since then, the automobile has probably been the key technological factor to make feasible the separation of residence, shopping, recreation and work. It should also be noted that construction of an extensive urban highway system, again subsidized by the Federal government, simultaneously encouraged the use of the automobile and made more land reasonably accessible (in terms of cost and proximity to the central city) for the decentralizing population. Finally, the decentralization of jobs and commercial establishments also stimulated, and has been stimulated by, the population spread.[5] As a result of these trends, suburban communities have experienced considerable population growth while many large cities have experienced a leveling off or an actual decline in population. This does not mean that migration into cities has ceased; it means that the exodus has been stronger than the immigration.

III. Metropolitanization as a Sorting Process

The basic population trends carry important implications for urban education. For example, the rapid increase of population in suburban areas, particularly of married couples with young children, put a tremendous strain on the educational facilities available in those areas and was responsible, in part, for the large capital expenditures of suburban school districts during the 1950's. These population trends take on even greater significance for the education function in both suburbs and central cities when they are examined in relation to such factors as race, income, educational attainment and the racial composition of the school population. Examined in these terms, it becomes apparent that the redistribution of population within metropolitan areas has not occurred on a random basis. The population shift not only involves numbers of people, it also constitutes a sorting-out

---

[5] The factors spurring metropolitan decentralization are dealt with in considerable detail in the following works: Richard Dewey, "Peripheral Expansion in Milwaukee County," *The American Journal of Sociology* (May, 1948), pp. 417-422; Robert C. Wood, *Suburbia: Its People and Their Politics* (Boston: Houghton Mifflin Co., 1958); William Dobriner (ed.), *The Suburban Community* (New York: G. P. Putnam's Sons, 1958); William Dobriner, *Class in Suburbia* (Englewood Cliffs: Prentice-Hall, Inc., 1963); Edgar M. Hoover and Raymond Vernon, *Anatomy of a Metropolis* (Garden City, New York: Doubleday and Company, Inc., 1962); Raymond Vernon, *The Myth and Reality of Our Urban Problems* (Cambridge: Joint Center for Urban Studies, MIT-Harvard, 1962); and York Willbern, *The Withering Away of the City* (University, Alabama: University of Alabama Press, 1964).

process. In general, it is the poor, less educated, black rural Americans who are migrating to and remaining in the core city, and the higher income, better educated whites who are fleeing to suburbia, although this description must be qualified somewhat in terms of the size and age of the central city as well as the region of the country in which it is located. The larger and older the city, however, the more accurate is this description.[6]

Table 3 illustrates this process in relation to the emerging racial composition of large central cities. The table shows that all of the 15

TABLE 3

White and Negro Population Changes in 15 Largest Cities, 1950-1960 and Estimates of Negro Population in 1965

	White Population		Negro Population			
	1960 (000)	Per cent Change Since 1950	1960 (000)	Per cent Change Since 1950	Per cent of 1960 Total	Estimated Per cent of 1965 Total
New York	6,641	− 7	1,088	46	14	18
Chicago	2,713	−13	813	65	23	28
Los Angeles[a]	2,391	−19	344	96	12	17
Philadelphia	1,407	−13	529	41	26	31
Detroit	1,183	−24	482	61	29	34
Baltimore	611	−16	326	45	35	38
Houston	721	53	215	72	23	23
Cleveland	623	−19	251	70	29	34
Washington	345	−33	412	47	54	66
St. Louis	534	−24	214	39	29	36
Milwaukee	676	10	62	187	8	11
San Francisco[b]	875	−14	158	74	14	21
Boston	629	−17	63	58	9	13
Dallas	548	46	129	127	19	21
New Orleans	393	1	234	29	37	41

[a] Includes Long Beach.
[b] Includes Oakland.
Source: U.S. Bureau of the Census, *U.S. Census of Population: 1960, Selected Area Reports, Standard Metropolitan Statistical Areas*, Table I. Estimates for 1965 are from *Report of the National Advisory Commission on Civil Disorders* (New York: Bantam Book Edition, 1968), p. 248.

---

[6] For a discussion of these differences in size and region, see: Advisory Commission on Intergovernmental Relations, *Metropolitan Social and Economic Disparities: Implications for Intergovernmental Relations in Central Cities and Suburbs* (Washington, D.C.: U.S. Government Printing Office, 1965).

largest central cities experienced a considerable increase in Negro population between 1950 and 1960, regardless of whether or not they lost population since 1950. In addition, 11 out of the 15 cities underwent a simultaneous loss of white population. Again, regional differences exist, but as the last column shows, large cities are increasingly inhabited by black citizens. Indeed, estimates for 1965 indicate that, since 1960, the black proportion of the population increased in all of the major cities in the nation.[7]

The result of this process is a growing concentration of so-called "high-cost citizens" in central cities.[8] These are citizens who, because of their social and economic needs, place enormous public demands on central city governments. One characteristic of these citizens is their consistently higher level of unemployment (and underemployment) compared to suburbanites. A recent analysis of unemployment rates in central city ghetto areas contrasted to the surrounding suburban rings indicated at least twice as much unemployment in the central cities.[9] There is evidence that unemployment rates among young black males is as high as 32 per cent in some cities.[10] Thus, it is not surprising that big cities have a larger proportion of families with incomes below $3,000 (an often-used poverty level) than do their suburbs (15.4 per cent compared to 8.9 per cent). Even more significant, given the population trends discussed, is the fact that the percentage of central city black families with incomes under $3,000 in 1964 was more than double the white proportion—29 per cent compared to 12 per cent.[11] Consequently, if recent population shifts continue, and there is little evidence that they will not, it is clear that many large cities will become the principal containers of poverty-stricken families, and that the income disparity between cities and suburbs will increase. This trend is suggested by the fact that the gap between central city and outside-central city family income was $767 in 1959 and $1,075 in 1964, an increase of $308.[12]

---

[7] *Congressional Quarterly Weekly Report* (August 26, 1966), pp. 1860-1862.

[8] Advisory Commission on Intergovernmental Relations, *Fiscal Balance in the American Federal System: Metropolitan Fiscal Disparities, Vol. 2* (Washington, D.C.: U.S. Government Printing Office, 1967), p. 5.

[9] U.S. Department of Labor, *Manpower Report of the President* (Washington, D.C.: U.S. Government Printing Office, 1967), p. 75.

[10] U.S. Department of Labor, *Recent Trends in Social and Economic Conditions of Negroes in the United States* (Washington, D.C.: U.S. Government Printing Office, 1968), p. 14.

[11] U.S. Bureau of the Census, *Current Population Reports, Series P-60, No. 48,* "Income in 1964 of Families and Unrelated Individuals by Metropolitan-Non Metropolitan Residence" (Washington, D.C.: U.S. Government Printing Office, 1966).

[12] Advisory Commission in Intergovernmental Relation, *Fiscal Balance . . .*, p. 43.

It has also been documented that, because of population shifts, cities shoulder an extraordinarily high share of public-assistance case loads. A recent report states: "With only one exception among the cities for which such data could be developed, the city's share of its state's welfare case load is dramatically larger than its share of the state's population." For example, while Baltimore contained only one-fourth of Maryland's population in 1966, it contained about three-fourths of the state's recipients of aid to families with dependent children.[13]

Educational attainment is often viewed as the primary means for overcoming some of the disadvantages encountered by city residents. But here again we find a gap between city and suburban populations. In 1960, about 41 per cent of city inhabitants over 25 years of age completed four years of high school, while 51 per cent was the comparable figure for suburbanites. These differences are likely to become even greater, because only about 28 per cent of adult blacks living in cities have completed a high school education. In other words, somewhere near 70 per cent of central city black youngsters may have parents with less than a high school education. Indeed, about 61 per cent of blacks 25 years old and over had no more than eight years of schooling in 1960.[14]

IV. Population Changes and Educational Implications

The redistribution of population had its most immediate and visible impact on the suburban areas of the nation. The rapid influx of middle-class and, later, lower middle-class migrants into the suburban ring placed a strain on existing governmental services and created demands for additional services. Suburban school districts felt the impact of the expanded population in a compounded manner because the growth in school population outstripped general population growth, and some of the newcomers placed considerable emphasis on establishing a quality educational system. These educational demands were made, in numerous instances, on essentially new residential communities which often lacked an industrial or commercial tax base to supplement the property tax effort of homeowners. In the more established suburban communities and in formerly rural communities, the new families not only encountered a weak tax base, but quite often a more aged and/or less educationally-oriented population which was not anxious to finance

---

[13] *Ibid.*, p. 40.
[14] U.S. Bureau of the Census, *U.S. Census of Population: 1960 General Social and Economic Characteristics.*

sprawling new school buildings which included what some of them considered "educational frills."[15]

Although most suburbs were generally able to meet the educational challenge by building the necessary physical facilities, providing a student transportation system and recruiting a quality teaching staff, these accomplishments were not made in the absence of political controversy. In fact, much of the political conflict that has occurred in suburban communities has often centered on school issues, since educational expenditures ordinarily account for about half of the total community budget and suburbanites have indicated (at least initially) a deeper personal interest in education than in other governmental services.[16] The metropolitanization of the population, then, both in its magnitude and qualitative features, has strongly influenced the nature of school politics in suburbia. Chapter 3 deals more specifically with the kinds of political controversies that have emerged, the management of those controversies, and with the important actors, the outcomes, and the nature of educational decision-making in suburban communities.

The initial concentration of public attention on suburban schools tended to obscure the implications of suburban expansion for central city schools. It has more recently become clear that suburbanization, by draining the higher income, white families and much economic activity from the cities, produced more serious educational and political problems for city school districts than it did for suburban districts. Fundamentally, the decentralization of population has dramatically changed the clientele of city school systems. From the perspective of city schoolmen, a disproportionate and rapidly growing segment of the school population is "educationally disadvantaged." These students are "disadvantaged" in terms of the income level and educational background of their parents, their family composition, and their general home and neighborhood environments. The educational problems generated by such students are succinctly described by Martin Deutsch, who writes:

> Among children who come from lower-class socially impoverished circumstances, there is a high proportion of school failure, school dropouts, reading and learning disabilities, as well as life adjustment problems. This means not only that these children grow up poorly equipped academically, but also that the effectiveness of the school as a major institution for socialization is diminished.

---

[15] Dobriner, *Class in Suburbia*, pp. 127-140.
[16] Wood, *Suburbia: Its People and Their Politics*, pp. 186-194.

The thesis here is that the lower-class child enters the school situation so poorly prepared to produce what the school demands that initial failures are almost inevitable, and the school experience becomes negatively rather than positively reinforced. Thus, the child's experience in school does nothing to counteract the invidious influences to which he is exposed in his slum, and sometimes segregated neighborhood.[17]

Although both white and black students are found in the "disadvantaged" category, blacks are disproportionately represented because of the socio-economic characteristics of the group as a whole. Consequently, as black students become a larger and larger proportion of the student population in a city, the school system experiences an almost equivalent increase in what most school officials view as "disadvantaged" students. The recent population changes have had, from the perspective of professional educators, exactly this impact. In fact, the growth of black population has probably had a more severe impact on city school systems than on other city institutions, since black student increases outstrip total black population growth in most cities. This ratio results from the fact that the black population has a higher birth rate, is relatively younger, has more children of school age, and is less able to make use of private and parochial schools than whites. A recent study reveals that, in the 20 largest cities, about four out of ten white students are enrolled in nonpublic schools, compared to only one out of ten black students.[18] As a result of all these factors, blacks now constitute a majority of public school students in nine of the fifteen largest American cities (see Table 4) and will probably be a majority in all fifteen within a decade. Therefore, devising a successful educational program for black students and other low-income students is the major problem confronting city school systems.

Many commentators have argued convincingly that the problem of providing such students with an adequate education is magnified by the fact that the school system itself is ill-equipped to meet the needs of low-income students. They maintain that the schools have failed miserably in their primary mission of providing all students, regardless of background, with opportunities to realize their maximum potential. Instead of helping students to overcome initial deficiencies, the schools are viewed as institutions which have intensified handicaps. City school systems have been accused not only of being run by middle-class

---

[17] Martin Deutsch, "The Disadvantaged Child and the Learning Process," in A. Harry Passow (ed.), *Education in Depressed Areas* (New York: Teachers College, Columbia University, 1963), p. 163.

[18] Robert Dentler, "Big City School Desegregation: Trends and Methods," National Conference on Equal Educational Opportunity, November, 1967, p. 3.

TABLE 4

Negroes as Proportion of School Enrollment
in 15 Largest Cities, 1960-1966

	Negroes as Per cent of School Enrollment 1960	Negroes as Per cent of School Enrollment 1966
New York	20	31
Chicago	44	53
Los Angeles	21	41
Philadelphia	50	59
Detroit	46	55
Baltimore	57	64
Houston	28	34
Cleveland	47	54
Washington, D.C.	83	91
St. Louis	50	63
San Francisco	36	57
Milwaukee	17	26
Boston	16	29
Dallas	22	28
New Orleans	58	66

Source: U.S. Bureau of Census, *U.S. Census of Population and Housing, 1960* and U.S. Commission on Civil Rights, *Racial Isolation in the Public Schools* (Washington, D.C.: U.S. Government Printing Office, 1967).

whites who have little understanding of teaching lower-class students (particularly black students), but of containing significant numbers of incompetent and racist teachers, utilizing irrelevant curricula material, allocating fewer resources to schools attended predominantly by black students, and of being substantially incapable of instituting meaningful innovations to meet the needs of their changing clientele.[19]

Whether the background of low-income black students or the internal characteristics of city school systems is the primary contributor to many students' educational failure is an issue explored later in this book. It is sufficient to note at this point that practically all reform proposals would involve a substantial increase in the fiscal resources allocated to city schools. Some commentators argue that a doubling or

[19] See, for example: Patricia Sexton, *Education and Income* (New York: Viking Press, 1961); Charles E. Silberman, *Crisis in Black and White* (New York: Vintage Book, 1964), Chap. IX; Kenneth B. Clark, *Dark Ghetto* (New York: Harper, 1965); Jonathan Kozol, *Death at an Early Age* (New York: Bantam Books, Inc., 1967) and Marilyn Gittell and T. Edward Hollander, *Six Urban School Districts* (New York: Frederick A. Praeger, 1968).

tripling of per-pupil expenditures is necessary for any meaningful solution to the problem. In this respect, it is important to examine the impact of metropolitanization on the fiscal strength of cities and their school districts.

V. Metropolitanism and Fiscal Resources

The educational problems confronting large cities are accentuated by their lack of ample resources for dealing with their difficulties. The metropolitan process has not only redistributed the population in a manner that presents central cities with a growing school population requiring special and innovative educational programs, but has simultaneously operated to weaken the local fiscal base upon which the schools rely for support.

It has already been noted that the central city component of the metropolitan area population has lower income levels than does the population in the surrounding suburbs. This pattern is particularly significant because it has become increasingly apparent that family income is the single most important variable in explaining the expenditure levels of a community for both educational and noneducational services.[20] To a large extent, the available income determines the ability of a governmental unit to meet the service requirements of its population. Central cities are simply losing ground in this respect, while their public service needs are simultaneously increasing.

Complementing this disparity in income levels is the fact that economic activities have also decentralized from the core city to the suburbs. Evidence of this trend can be found by examining the distribution of economic activity within specific metropolitan areas over time. For example, an investigation of the proportion of manufacturing carried on in the central city sector of 12 large metropolitan areas demonstrates that the central city percentage has declined over the past three decades, particularly in the post-World War II period. Whereas the 12 cities accounted, on the average, for 66.1 per cent of manufacturing employment in 1929, this proportion decreased to 60.8 per cent by 1947 and then declined to less than half (48.9 per cent) by 1958.[21]

---

[20] Alan K. Campbell and Seymour Sacks, *Metropolitan America: Fiscal Patterns and Governmental Systems* (New York: The Free Press, 1967).

[21] See Raymond Vernon, *The Changing Economic Function of the Central City* (New York: Committee for Economic Development, 1960); and U.S. Bureau of the Census, *Census of Manufacturing*, 1958. The cities include: Baltimore, Boston, Chicago, Cincinnati, Cleveland, Detroit, Los Angeles-Long Beach, New York, Philadelphia, Pittsburgh, St. Louis, and San Francisco-Oakland.

A similar pattern has been discovered in retail sales. A recent report found that:

> . . . retail sales increased in 24 of the 37 largest central city areas and declined in 13 areas, for an overall increase of 4.8 per cent (during 1958-1963). Outside areas increased on the average of 45.5 per cent, substantially in excess of the increase in population and income. The large increase outside the central cities represented a shift in the location of retail activity [and] represented a decline in the importance of the central cities as retail centers when compared either to the suburban areas or the rest of the nation.[22]

This report concluded that the historical dominance of the central city and its business district over metropolitan retail activity is clearly on the decline.

The patterns for manufacturing, employment, and retail sales reflect the fact that economic activity, like population, has migrated from the central city outward.[23] This push for dispersal is related to a number of factors, including the need for physical space, the introduction of new industrial processes, the ascendance of the automobile and truck as means of transportation and shipping, the building of vast highway systems, and the spreading of the population throughout the metropolis.[24] There is little evidence to suggest that this trend is slowing down or reversing, despite such programs as urban renewal and model cities.

The impact of economic decentralization on the tax base of the central city has been widely discussed. As industries continue to move outward, taxable assessed valuation (the source of local property taxes) has barely held its own in many cities and has actually declined in several large cities. In a recent five-year period, the per cent changes in taxable assessed valuation for seven large cities were as follows: Baltimore, −10.5 per cent; Boston, −1.2 per cent; Buffalo, −1.0 per cent; Detroit, 2.0 per cent; St. Louis, +1.1 per cent; Philadelphia, +2.8 per cent; and Cleveland, −3.4 per cent.[25] These changes in taxable valuation do not yield the fiscal resources required to deal with the public service needs facing these urban centers.

Translated into educational terms, the recent performance of the local tax base in many large cities has not kept pace with the growth

---

[22] Advisory Commission on Intergovernmental Relations, *Fiscal Balance. . . ,* *op. cit.,* p. 50.

[23] Dorothy K. Newman, "The Decentralization of Jobs," *Monthly Labor Review* (May, 1967), pp. 7-13.

[24] Edgar M. Hoover and Raymond Vernon, *Anatomy of a Metropolis* (Garden City, N.Y.: Doubleday and Company, Inc., 1962).

[25] The Research Council of the Great Cities Program for School Improvement, *The Challenge of Financing Public Schools in Great Cities,* Chicago, 1964.

or nature of the school population in these cities. Indeed, an examination of the per-pupil taxable valuation over a five-year period shows that ten large cities out of fourteen experienced an actual decrease in this source of revenue. Since local property taxes are the most important source of local educational revenues (they contributed 52 per cent of all education revenue in 1968), large city schools find it increasingly difficult to meet ordinary educational needs, let alone support special educational programs required by the shifting population distribution.

TABLE 5

Five-Year Changes in Per Pupil Taxable Assessed Valuation
in 14 Large Cities, 1964

	Per cent of Change over a Five-Year Period[a]	
	City	State (minus cities listed)
Baltimore	−19.3	10.2
Boston	− 5.3	not available
Buffalo	− 8.6	26.1
Chicago	− 6.0	− 0.2
Cleveland	− 9.9	4.2
Detroit	− 5.7	3.4
Houston	− 2.8	18.9
Los Angeles	5.1	5.6
Milwaukee	− 9.6	− 1.1
New York City	32.4	26.1
Philadelphia	− 0.6	13.6
Pittsburgh	2.2	13.6
St. Louis	−10.6	3.1
San Francisco	5.9	5.6

[a] Change is for the most recent five-year period for which data are available.
Source: Research Council of the Great Cities Program for School Improvement, *The Challenge of Financing Public Schools in Great Cities*, Chicago, 1964.

An additional factor weighs against the fiscal capacity of central cities to meet their pressing educational needs. The intensification of urbanization and metropolitanization has resulted in an ever-increasing demand for a wider range of and higher quality in public services. These demands are particularly great in large cities where the necessity for providing a wide variety of welfare, public safety, health, sanitation, traffic control, pollution control, and street maintenance services

TABLE 6

Fiscal Characteristics for Central City and
Outside Central City Areas, 35 Sample SMSA's: 1962
(Mean Per Capita)

	Central City	Outside Central City	Difference Central City— Outside Central City
Total Expenditures	$ 229.66	$ 253.68	$− 24.59
Education Expenditures	67.96	127.24	− 59.28
(Per Student Expenditures)	414.46	559.42	−144.96
Noneducation Expenditures	161.70	126.44	+ 35.26
Locally Raised Tax Revenue	143.33	115.90	+ 27.43
Intergovernmental Aid	67.68	55.39	+ 12.29
State Education Aid	20.73	37.66	− 16.93
(Per Student)	124.92	165.54	− 40.62
Median Family Income	5,943.00	6,707.00	−764.00

Source: Computed from U.S. Bureau of Census, *Census of Government,* 1962
(Washington, D.C.: U.S. Government Printing Office, 1964).

has been most pressing. The fact that central cities have responded to these demands is reflected in the data of Table 6. An investigation of the fiscal patterns in thirty-five Standard Metropolitan Statistical Areas revealed that for the year 1962, the central cities in these areas were spending $35.26 more per capita on noneducational expenditures than were the communities in the outlying areas. Unfortunately for the central city educational systems, this relationship was not found in educational expenditures. The cities spent $59.28 less per capita on education than did the suburban communities. This difference in educational and noneducational expenditures is no doubt related to the fact that cities, unlike many suburban communities, must provide a wider range of traditional municipal services. The cost and number of such services tend to increase with the size and density of a community and to consume a larger proportion of the budget in major cities where services are provided for non-resident commuters as well as for the growing number of "high-cost citizens." It is reasonable to suggest that this "municipal overburden," as it is often called, is supported to some extent at the expense of the education function.[26]

---

[26] David C. Ranney, *School Government and the Determinants of the Fiscal Support for Large City Education Systems* (Unpublished Doctoral dissertation, Syracuse University, 1966).

The figures in Table 6 also show that the central cities were supporting these expenditure levels by taxes that were $27.43 per capita higher than in areas outside the cities. The cities received $12.29 per capita more in total intergovernmental aid but, most importantly, $16.93 *less* per capita in education than did the suburban areas, where income was higher. On a per-student basis, the cities received $125 from the state compared to $166 for the suburbs—a difference of $41 for each student. In other words, not only were central cities pressed to support a large array of services by a relatively shrinking tax base, but they taxed themselves more heavily to do so and received less intergovernmental education aid than did the wealthier communities in their metropolitan area. This fiscal pattern borders on the ironic when one realizes that central city education systems must compete in the same labor market with suburban school districts which have higher income levels and receive a greater amount of state aid. In fact, the state aid system actually works to intensify rather than to equalize the disparities between what Americans spend on city students and suburban students.

The multitude of fiscal difficulties which the central cities face has resulted in a lower per-student expenditure in the cities than in the suburbs. This was not always the case. A study of the 37 largest metropolitan areas found that, in 1957, central city schools were spending $312 per pupil, and suburbs, $303. By 1962, however, these same cities spent, on an average, $64 less than the suburbs, $375 compared to $438. And by 1964, the gap had widened to $124 per pupil $449 compared to $573.[27]

This considerable difference in expenditure per student between central city and suburb would be serious even if the educational problems were the same for each, but indeed, the problems are not the same, since many city students require special and costly compensatory education programs. The ability of city school systems to support such programs through locally-raised funds is simply declining. Consequently, many city school systems face a double crisis emanating from the changing nature of their clientele and a serious shortage of fiscal resources.

VI. Summary

In summary, then, the metropolitanization of American society has had a significant impact on school districts in both the suburban and

---

[27] Advisory Commission, *Fiscal Balance. . . , op. cit.,* p. 66.

the city components of the metropolis. The population flow flooded the suburbs with millions of young families who carried with them high educational aspirations for their children, and drained the core cities of the higher income, more highly educated adults and white students. This population distribution left the city school districts with a new clientele of what educators viewed as "disadvantaged" students and, as will be discussed later, a serious *de facto* segregation and legitimacy problem. The simultaneous dispersal of economic activity has helped to build up the tax base of *some* suburban communities, but has weakened the cities' fiscal capacity for meeting both their educational and noneducational service needs. Consequently, while the metropolitan process initially presented suburban schools with an education crisis, a more critical set of problems has developed and is currently confronting city school systems. The following two chapters examine these developments in suburbia and the city in greater detail.

School Politics in Suburbia

3

I. Schools in the Suburban Setting

As noted in the previous chapter, the movement of young, essentially middle-class, white families from the city to the surrounding area is the basic characteristic of post-World War II suburbanization. The outward migration of this segment of the city population has been largely responsible for the rapid multiplication and growth of communities ringing large cities. While popular accounts of suburbanization portray suburbia as a homogeneous mass, it is important to note the diversity found in and among these fringe communities. Gradually, the view of suburbia as simply a string of "bedroom communities" has been altered to include the recreational, educational, manufacturing, and working-class suburbs.[1] This recognition of suburban diversity, however, should not be overstressed to the point where it obscures the basic fact that the suburbs which exemplified post-World War II

---

[1] For example, see: Maurice R. Stein, *The Eclipse of Community* (New York: Harper and Row, 1960), Chapters 9 and 12; Bennett M. Berger, *Working Class Suburb* (Berkeley: University of California Press, 1960); William M. Dobriner, *Class in Suburbia* (Englewood Cliffs: Prentice-Hall, Inc., 1963); Leo F. Schnore, "The Social and Economic Characteristics of American Suburbs," *The Sociological Quarterly*, Vol. 40 (Spring, 1963), 122-134.

suburbanization and which experienced the most rapid population growth in the decade 1950-1960 were essentially residential communities.[2] These residential suburbs provide the most relevant comparison to cities in terms of city-suburban disparities, since the socio-economic characteristics of their inhabitants differ most distinctly from central city residents.

TABLE 7

Social and Economic Characteristics of 25 Largest Cities
and Their Residential Suburbs, 1960

	Central Cities	Residential Suburbs	Differences: Suburbs-Cities
Population Growth 1950-1960	12%	27%	+ 15%
Per cent Negro	20%	2%	− 18%
Per cent Completed High School	41%	56%	+ 15%
Per cent White Collar	45%	59%	+ 14%
Median Family Income	$5,974	$8,210	+$2,236
Cumulative Fertility Rate*	1,531	1,759	+228
Per cent One-Family Units	53%	76%	+ 23%

* Children ever born per 1,000 women 15-44 years old.
Source: Central city data was computed from U.S. Bureau of the Census, *U.S. Census of Population: 1960; General Social and Economic Characteristics; U.S. Census of Housing: 1960.* The suburban data is from Schnore, *op. cit.*

Table 7 indicates the magnitude of these city-suburban disparities by comparing the 25 largest cities with their residential suburbs. In sum, the suburbs have far fewer Negro residents, a larger number of adult high school graduates and white collar workers, a substantially higher median family income, a higher fertility rate, and a greater percentage of one-family homes than do cities. The suburban population varies in other important aspects from city residents. Suburbs, for

---

[2] In an analysis of the suburbs surrounding the 25 largest cities, it was found that the 102 employing-type suburbs had undergone an average growth of 6 per cent from 1950 to 1960, while the 99 residential-type suburbs had grown an average of 27 per cent. See Leo Schnore, *ibid.*

example, generally have, in addition to higher fertility ratios, higher percentages of married couples, higher percentages of primary families, a lower median age, lower percentages of separated couples, lower ratios of quasi-household residents to population in households, and lower percentages of women in the labor force.[3]

The combination of these socio-economic attributes represents an abstract index to the sociological concept of "life style." This concept refers to the general way of life which characterizes various individuals or groups. A phrase often utilized to describe the life style of suburbanites is "child-oriented familism." A typical description reads: "the move to the suburbs expresses an attempt to find a location in which to conduct family life which is more suitable than that offered by central cities . . . persons moving to the suburbs are principally those who have chosen familism as an important element of their life styles."[4] Indeed, the scholars who have conducted the most detailed investigation of suburban culture arrived at the conclusion that: "In Crestwood Heights the major institutional focus is upon child-rearing."[5]

This emphasis on family life, particularly as it centers around the child, carries important implications for suburban schools. In the first place, many parents who decide to move to suburbia often consider the reputation of the schools in selecting a particular suburban community. Once they have chosen a community and settled in it, much of their interest in community affairs centers on the key public service: the schools.[6] Although somewhat over-dramatized, the following statement suggests the paramount position of schools in the more affluent residential suburbs:

> A member of the Board of Education, in a speech to the community, stated that Crestwood Heights and the school are one and the same; that the Crestwood Heights social and municipal organization virtually exists to make the school possible; that the school is the center of the community, and that everything revolves around and within it. He

---

[3] Dobriner, *op. cit.*, p. 19.

[4] Wendell Bell, "Social Choice, Life Styles and Suburban Residence" in William Dobriner (ed.), *The Suburban Community* (New York: G. P. Putnam's Sons, 1958), p. 231.

[5] J. R. Seeley, R. A. Sim, E. W. Loosley, *Crestwood Heights: A Study of the Culture of Suburban Life* (New York: John Wiley & Sons Inc., 1956), p. 4. Although Crestwood Heights is a Canadian suburb, it is very similar to American middle class suburbs.

[6] Robert C. Wood, *Suburbia: Its People and Their Politics* (Boston: Houghton Mifflin Company, 1958), pp. 186-87.

spoke a little as a Catholic priest in some French Canadian parish might about his church. Summing up the relation of the school to Crestwood Heights, he said 'The school is all we have.'[7]

The importance of schools may be demonstrated more concretely by examining the relative proportion of fiscal resources devoted to education in suburban communities. An analysis dealing with the fiscal patterns of the 12 largest metropolitan areas in 1957 revealed that the central cities in those areas were spending, on the average, approximately one-fourth of their total public expenditures on education whereas the suburbs were allocating one-half of their budgets to education and were spending about $28 more per person on schools than the cities.[8] A follow-up inquiry (see Table 8) indicated that by 1962, the suburbs continued to devote one-half of their expenditures to education while the cities still spent only about one-fourth of their funds on schools. More significantly, while this relative relationship remained constant, the absolute difference between suburban and city school expenditures per capita increased from $28 to $62. As was noted in the previous chapter, the suburbs lagged slightly behind the cities on per-pupil expenditures in the 37 largest metropolitan areas in 1957, but forged considerably ahead by 1964. This relative growth in suburban expenditures is even more impressive, as Sacks and Ranney note, when it is realized that "suburban school enrollments grew between 1957 and 1962 at almost twice the rate of their central city counterparts."[9]

From both qualitative and quantitative perspectives, then, the schools in suburban communities occupy a position of utmost importance. They often act as a population magnet; they are at the center of community interest and activity because of the importance placed on the education function; and more public funds are poured into them than into any other governmental service. For these reasons, the school district stands at the very core of the governmental system in many suburban communities. Because the schools do occupy such a central position in suburbs, professional educators in numerous

---

[7] J. R. Seeley, *et al.*, *op. cit.*, p. 234. Also see James B. Conant, *Slums and Suburbs: A Commentary on Schools in Metropolitan Areas* (New York: New American Library, 1961), Chapter IV, "The College-Oriented Suburbs" for a discussion of the great pressure exerted on suburan schools to prepare students for high-quality universities.

[8] Harvey E. Brazer, "Some Fiscal Implications of Metropolitanism" in Guthrie S. Birkhead (ed.), *Metropolitan Issues: Social Governmental, Fiscal* (Syracuse: Maxwell Graduate School, Syracuse University, 1962), p. 72.

[9] Seymour Sacks and David C. Ranney, "Suburban Education: A Fiscal Analysis," *Urban Affairs Quarterly* (September, 1966), pp. 103-119.

TABLE 8
Per Capita Expenditures for Education as a Per Cent of Total Expenditures, Central Cities and Outside Central City: 1957 and 1962

	1957				1962			
	CC Educa. Expend.	% of Total	OCC Educa. Expend.	% of Total	CC Educa. Expend.	% of Total	OCC Educa. Expend.	% of Total
New York	$ 63	24%	$106	47%	$ 77	22%	$194	55%
Newark	74	30	106	50	94	32	112	43
Chicago	48	24	82	56	66	27	113	45
Los Angeles	95	36	93	46	101	33	175	47
Long Beach	115	34	93	46	86	33	175	47
Philadelphia	49	30	72	52	55	26	106	56
Detroit	62	30	114	59	94	36	128	49
San Francisco	62	28	112	49	69	22	172	49
Baltimore	59	29	71	50	81	28	113	55
Cleveland	50	29	85	48	65	29	114	45
Minneapolis	59	27	97	47	61	28	157	52
St. Paul	51	27	97	47	58	23	157	52
St. Louis	45	28	71	56	55	28	101	57
Boston	48	17	70	38	50	18	101	41
Pittsburgh	41	21	66	49	51	30	96	51
Mean	$ 61'	28%	$ 89	49%	$ 72	28%	$134	50%

Source: The 1957 data is from Brazer, *op. cit.* The 1962 data was computed from the U.S. Bureau of the Census, *1962 Census of Governments.*

communities have found it particularly difficult to defend their claims to educational expertise and to insulate the schools from political conflict.

The sources of suburban school conflict vary, of course, from community to community. However, it is possible to identify some common factors which contribute to the controversies that have occurred. One of these factors has already been mentioned—the rapid growth of educational expenditures in suburban school districts. Intimately related to increased expenditures is rapid population growth and population diversity within suburban communities. The combination of these three factors quite often underpins the most heated strife in suburban schools. A closely related issue concerns the question of school-district consolidation with other suburban districts and the central city school system. This latter issue is usually raised in connection with the problem of fiscal strain or, in a few instances, the question of integration. In fact, the issue of "racial balance" in suburban schools is one of the more recent sources of discord.

To demonstrate how these factors influence the nature of school politics in suburbia, one must rely on case studies drawn from various sources, since there is a lack of comparative literature on the topic. Consequently, we utilize in the following section several case studies of specific suburban communities to illustrate the kinds of political conflicts which have emerged, the sources of conflict, and the impact of these events on the educators' desires to guard closely their control over educational decision-making, to protect their professional status, to shield the schools from "politics," and to retain public confidence.

II. Suburban Schools and Political Conflict: The Levittown Cases

Levittown, Long Island, is clearly a prototype of the spanking-new, mass-produced postwar suburbs.[10] It was the first, and most famous, of the three Levittowns built by Levitt and Sons, Inc., in the Northeastern section of the country. Although the contractors originally planned, in 1947, to erect a subdivision of 2,000 units to be rented for $60 a month to returning veterans, they soon discovered that the market-demand for single family-owned houses was so great that, by 1951, they had actually built, on a former potato farm, a completely new

---

10 This description of Levittown, Long Island, and its school crisis is based upon Dobriner, *Class in Suburbia*, pp. 85-126; Joseph F. Maloney, '*The Lonesome Train*' in Levittown (University of Alabama, University of Alabama Press, ICP Case 39, 1958); and National Education Association of United States and Ethical Practices Committee of the New York State Teachers Association. *Levittown, New York,* January, 1962.

town for 15,000 families which included schools, 14 park-playgrounds, a $150,000 swimming pool for each 2,000 families, and a $200,000 community center.

Drawing over half of its inhabitants from New York City, the community of several hundred in 1947 exploded to about 65,000 people by 1960, one-third of whom were under 10 years of age. The rapid growth in population put an extraordinary strain on school facilities. In 1948 there were 40 students and 2 teachers in the single community school; the tax rate per $100 of assessed property valuation was $00.73; and the school budget was $22,550. By 1960, the school population had climbed to over 18,000 students and 678 teachers, who were housed in 15 new school buildings. The tax rate had increased about eight-fold, from $00.73 to $6.45 per $100.[11]

Since Levittown had no industry to tax and very little business property, the local portion of the education bill which supported these changes was paid almost exclusively by private home owners. Virtually every year the new home owners were presented with an increasing property tax bill, a factor which many of them had not anticipated when they decided to become suburban home owners. With a median family income of $7,467 in 1959, the community was clearly composed of families with modest incomes who viewed the increasing educational costs as problematic. Indeed, Dobriner, Maloney, and the NEA special committee all concluded that the problem of meeting the growing educational costs which faced many Levittown families was the root of several bitter community conflicts.

Maloney describes the community as split into two broad groups. One group was particularly sensitive to the economic strain created by the expanding school system. They felt that educational expenses were rising too rapidly, and that the school system was spending the money on "unnecessary frills" rather than concentrating on basic teaching competence and on developing well-disciplined citizens. To lead the protest against what they felt were uneconomical school policies and lack of moral training, the group formed the Parents Association for Education, and challenged the school system on several issues. The other group, known as the Educational Association, generally backed the policies of the school board and administration and pushed for even greater educational expenditures. They felt that the emphasis on so-called "progressive education" was correct; they did not want disciplinary and moral training in the schools accentuated over intellectual development.

---

[11] Dobriner, *op. cit.*, p. 113.

These factions were grounded, to some extent, on religious differences, although there were members of the three major religious groups in both camps. Catholics, however, held prominent positions in the Parents Association for Education, while the most active and articulate members of the Educational Association were Jewish. Many of the Catholic leaders based their criticism of the school on their own parochial school backgrounds. They argued that, since nuns could prepare 40 or 50 students with a solid education in the 3 R's while also providing them with appropriate moral training, the Levittown public school system (there were no parochial schools in the community) could certainly save money by conducting larger classes and curtaining many of the so-called frills, such as bands, clubs, school psychologists and so forth. Some members of the Educational Association countered their suggestions by accusing the Catholics of attempting to turn the public schools into parochial schools. Maloney writes that:

'Beat the Catholic bloc' became the slogan for some of the extreme members of the E.A. Some of the minority group (the P.A.E.) countered with the accusations that the E.A. was controlled by atheistic Jewish leftwingers bent on subverting the children from being moral, disciplined Americans into being amoral, radical internationalists. These accusations and counter accusations added a bitter undercurrent to community consideration of school problems.[12]

During the period 1954-1955, this split became particularly serious over "The Lonesome Train" episode. This was the title of a recorded cantata that was being used in the lower elementary grades to teach children the many different ways music could be used to illustrate moods in a story. Several Levittown residents read an article in a monthly Catholic magazine which stated that the cantata had been written and scored by two Communists and that it contained blatant Communist propaganda.

When this accusation was brought to the attention of the superintendent of schools (a man who, in the eyes of many critics of the school system, was allied with the board members and the E.A. in support of "progressive education"), he ordered that there be no further use of the record until he could obtain a ruling from the State Education Department on its suitability. The State responded that the responsibility for selection of instructional material rests with the local district, and that while the State had a commission to deal with questionable textual material, it probably lacked jurisdiction over recordings. After receiv-

---

[12] Maloney, *op. cit.*, p. 3.

ing the information from the State, the superintendent held a meeting with the administrators in the system. It was decided that the schools would establish a policy that approval by professional educators, not community pressure, would determine the use of instructional material. The superintendent endorsed the recommendation made at the meeting and ordered that the record in question be made available again for teacher use. This action was taken without any public notice or communication with the citizens who had originally brought the matter to the attention of the superintendent.

For a while, nothing more was heard about "The Lonesome Train." A few months later, however, a citizen wrote a letter to the superintendent and to a local newspaper protesting some parodies on the song "Davey Crockett" which were written and sung in one of the schools. She felt that the parodies were derogatory to American heroes and were a threat to the children' patriotism. Her letter also revived the cantata issue, which within the next few weeks became a full-blown public controversy.

The superintendent publicly defended his action on the grounds that the inquiry at the State level revealed no evidence that the song was detrimental and that professional educators were best equipped to judge the appropriateness of educational material. A series of letters and public statements by citizens questioned the meaning of the superintendent's communications with the State. Eventually a review board was established to advise the superintendent on the suitability of instructional material. The board originally included one lay member, the president of the district's P.T.A. Council, and several teachers. Members of the Board of Education objected to this review board, however, and the one lay member was removed, to the dismay of the vocal critics.

As the review board deliberated about "The Lonesome Train," they were confronted with the dilemma of protecting the schools from arbitrary external pressure while simultaneously maintaining sufficient community confidence in the competence and patriotism of the educators.[13] After a great deal of internal debate, their findings were announced by the superintendent at a public Board of Education meeting. The review board had split, thus undermining the image of expert consensus educators like to project. One group decided that "the cantata, heard in its entirety by children and not torn to shreds by adults, is of value and interest when used as supplementary enrichment

---

[13] The deliberations of the review board are described in some detail by Maloney, *ibid.*, pp. 9-13.

material." The other group concluded that the cantata carried "a message that will unfavorably influence the minds of children . . . [It] . . . is clearly intended to be and is Communist propaganda."[14] Given these divergent views, the superintendent then made his own recommendation, which was that the record could still be used in the schools, but that accompanying its use, the teacher must provide additional information to illustrate how the material in the record was distorted. The Board of Education adopted his recommendation by a vote of four to two.

Obviously, the conflict was by no means resolved. Indeed, both the superintendent and the board members were criticized from both directions; some critics deplored the use of Communist propaganda in the schools and others protested that to label the cantata as a distortion before the students even heard it would impair their development of independent evaluation.

One of the dissenting Board members filed a suit with the State Commissioner of Education to have the record banned. While the Commissioner's decision was pending, campaigning began in the school district for the three Board seats which were up that year. Three of the candidates (all Catholics) backed the pending suit and were endorsed by the P.A.E. Their platform stressed the dangers of Communism, atheism, juvenile delinquency, and the need for greater economy in the schools. Two of the other three candidates (Jewish) were incumbents, who supported the superintendent and greater educational expenditures. They were attacked not only for being spendthrifts, but for being "soft" on Communism. The three opponents of the superintendent were elected and during the first new Board meeting they joined the old Board member (who at that time was elected president of the Board) in banning "The Lonesome Train" record from the Levittown schools.

Within six months the superintendent resigned his post, which remained vacant for an entire year. Other controversial issues, including a conflict over the separation of church and state and the defeat of a major bond issue for sorely-needed additional classrooms, continued to plague the school system, so that by 1960, the Levittown Teachers Association was actually operating a placement bureau for its members to find new teaching jobs in other school districts. Conflict grew so intense that the new superintendent was fired, two former Board members filed suits with the State to remove two current members, and the State Education Department and the National Educational Association launched a joint investigation of the entire school district.

---

[14] Quoted in *ibid.*, p. 13.

Needless to say, the desire on the part of educators to operate the schools in a placid, apolitical atmosphere where policy decisions are made with little citizen involvement or questioning was not achieved in Levittown. The lack of consensus might be interpreted as arising from the religious differences in the community; differences based on the divergent views of public education among Catholics, Protestants and Jews. There is little doubt that in part this was the case: many of the citizens interpreted the conflicts, and behaved accordingly, on religious grounds.[15] Dobriner points out, however, that there were members of all religious groups on the opposing sides of the various controversies and argues rather convincingly that social status is a more basic explanatory variable.[16] He notes, for example, that the general socio-economic status of the bulk of Levittown's Catholic population was blue collar, working class and argues that, while such people are interested in providing their children with a good fundamental education, they lack the intensive desire (and means) to fashion a first-rate school system according to middle-class standards. The Jewish and Protestant members of the community, on the other hand, had generally middle and upper-middle class characteristics and were anxious to provide their children with the best education possible, to enhance their opportunities for pursuing higher education.

The genesis of school conflict in Levittown, then, can be traced to the attraction to the fast-growing suburban community of families with diverse religious backgrounds who viewed the role of public schools differently, and of families with a substantial spread of social values and economic means. In fact, Dobriner presents data illustrating that during the decade 1950-1960, the heterogenity of the community increased considerably.[17] Although the suburb began as an essentially middle-class community, it attracted an increasing proportion of lower-middle and working-class families as it grew. The latter group brought modest educational aspirations for their children, and many of them had underestimated the costs of assuming home ownership in a new suburb. It is understandable, therefore, that many of them resisted supporting rising educational expenditures, particularly when they felt the money was being spent for "unnecessary education frills" and "subversive educational material."

Conflict over the level and distribution of school expenditures is not restricted, of course, to the case of Levittown, Long Island. Other writers have described suburban school strife arising from basic disagreement over the amount and allocation of school funds among

---

[15] See the quotes in Dobriner, pp. 118-119.
[16] *Ibid.*, pp. 120-26.
[17] *Ibid.*, pp. 85-112.

suburbanites with different social backgrounds and levels of wealth.[18] Indeed, it is quite interesting that in his study of Levittown, New Jersey, which is the most comprehensive study of a new postwar American suburb, Herbert Gans found this very pattern.[19] In this case, however, the first board of education and superintendent of the new school system were more traditional than in the Levittown, Long Island case. Gans describes the superintendent (who had been the rural county superintendent in the previous ten years) as "an Irish Catholic of lower-middle class origin . . . not in favor of progressive education, which struck him as totally permissive, [who] sought to combine what he called 'the teaching of traditional skills with individual treatment of children.' "[20] He was particularly concerned with average and slow-learning students, and felt that any extra energies and additional resources should be devoted to them, with the lowest priority given to bright students. While he felt that some students should be given an opportunity to prepare for higher education (state schools, such as he attended, not Ivy League types), he opposed overemphasis of college preparation in the curriculum and insisted that Levittown not attempt to copy upper-middle class suburbs such as Brookline and Scarsdale.

During the first year or so (1958), most Levittowners were so busy moving in and adjusting to the new suburb that few had time or the desire to make any serious complaints about the school system. However, it was not too long before the school system was confronted with what Gans refers to as "the revolt of the upper-middle class."[21] Some of the more affluent and highly educated residents of the community took issue with the system's policy that it would only admit children into kindergarten if they had reached the age of five by October 1. They wanted the deadline extended to December 31, and presented the board of education with a petition requesting the change. The board members reacted negatively (it was the first time they had ever encountered a petition) on the grounds that it would be unwise to place children in school before they were "naturally ready." They were somewhat resentful of the fact that some parents wanted their children

---

18 See, for example: Gary W. King, Walter E. Freeman and Christopher Sower, *Conflict Over Schools: A Sociological Analysis of a Suburban School Bond Election* (East Lansing, Michigan: Institute of Community Development and Services, Michigan State University, 1963) and Alan Rosenthal, "The Special Case of Public Education" in Richard T. Frost (ed.), *Cases in State and Local Government* (Englewood Cliffs, N.J.: Prentice-Hall, 1961), pp. 62-75.

19 Herbert J. Gans, *The Levittowners: Ways of Life and Politics in a New Suburban Community* (New York: Pantheon Books 1967), especially Chapter Five, "The New School System," pp. 86-103.

20 *Ibid.*, p. 87.

21 *Ibid.*, pp. 92-100.

in school at what they considered too young an age, not appreciating that the parents were already concerned about preparing their children for advanced education and professional careers.

After being rebuffed by the school board, the protesting parents organized the Citizens' Association for Public Schools (C.A.P.S.) and clashed with the board over the issue of overcrowding and class size. The community had attracted a greater proportion of large families with school-age children than had been anticipated; consequently, at least one of the elementary schools had classes with more than 35 children in them. The C.A.P.S. organization and the neighborhood PTA requested that class size in the school be reduced by busing some children to a less-crowded school, but the proposal was rejected. It appeared that the group would be repudiated a third time when they started to work on what they considered a more desirable curriculum for the schools. The superintendent quite unexpectedly, however, requested that several of them assist him on school matters.

It later became apparent that the superintendent's move represented an attempt by the administration to gain support in the community against a new and more widely-based set of school system critics. In a situation similar to that of Levittown, Long Island, a group began to coalesce around the issue of increasing school expenses and "educational frills." Once again, the controversy had a religious dimension, but here again it was fundamentally a social-class encounter.[22] The critics were able, in 1960, to defeat decisively the first school budget ever presented to the voters, and they jammed the school auditorium the next year to protest the proposed budget. Gans describes the meeting as "extremely bitter, with angry charges and exaggerated claims freely traded. The conflict was clearly between the haves and the have-nots, for when one lone budget supporter ended his speech, he was asked how much he was earning."[23] The budget was subsequently defeated, and three members of a so-called "Catholic slate," who campaigned on school economy, were elected to the board. The following year (1962), the voters again rejected the budget and the superintendent was asked to resign his post.

Political conflict, then, was very much an integral aspect of school governance in both of the Levittown suburbs. Although the conflict in the New Jersey community did not reach the intensity of that in the

---

[22] Gans wrote: "The most vocal attacks seemed to come from Catholics, who not only had lower incomes and more children than Protestants and Jewish Levittowners, but who were at that time also being asked to fund the building of a parochial school." *Ibid.*, p. 96.

[23] *Ibid.*, p. 98.

New York suburb, similar factors were operative in both instances. The rapid influx of young families with school age children necessitated ever-increasing school expenditures. The more affluent parents were quite willing to support the educational costs and some even pushed for greater expenditures. While both communities might be broadly defined as middle-class suburbs, they both attracted a substantial number of families who were relatively prosperous working class or new arrivals into the lower echelon of the middle class. Many of the working class had not anticipated the tax increases required to support a new school system. The combination of their tight financial situation and their values concerning education resulted in stiff opposition to the proponents of high education expenditures.

The possibilities of a clash between these two groups over educational policies was not minimized by the behavior of the school administrators. The rapid increase in school enrollment obviously put them in the difficult position of presenting larger and larger budgets. In both cases, the superintendents did not appear to recognize, until it was too late, the diverse population elements in the community and the different impacts that increased school expenditures would have on each of the groups. In other words, there was little recognition that the schools had competing political constituencies which perhaps called for planned citizen-participation in school policy-making. Whether providing citizens who represented various community elements with a meaningful role in the decision-making process would have prevented the high degree of controversy that emerged is, of course, difficult to predict. The significant point, however, is that schoolmen, particularly in new suburbs, must recognize that the schools are in a volatile political position and that political conflict is likely to occur. Therefore, established means for managing potential conflict should be consciously developed instead of adhering to the traditional view that the schools must remain apolitical. By assuming that the educational system can maintain such a posture, schoolmen may actually encourage development of the very kind of situation they wish to avoid.

III. Suburban Schools and Political Conflict: The New Trier Case

The preceding account illustrates the emergence of conflict surrounding school government in new, middle-class, heterogeneous suburbs which generally lacked established procedures for handling school controversy. This does not mean that older, more affluent suburban communities with institutional political processes have been immune to school strife emerging from the suburbanization process. The following case, which is based on Louis Massotti's study of the New Trier School District, exemplifies this point.[24]

The New Trier High School District, located in the northern suburban section of the Chicago metropolitan area, includes the upper-middle class suburbs of Glencoe, Winnetka, Kenilworth, Wilmette and Northfield. Massotti describes these communities as "all old (with the exception of Northfield) established, affluent 'bedroom' suburbs, populated in the main by upper-middle class and upper-class professional people and corporation executives who commute to the Chicago loop."[25] Since the turn of the century, these communities have supported a school system which over the years has gained the reputation of being one of the finest in the nation. In 1962, for example, the district spent over $1,000 per student, employed a highly educated and well-paid faculty, maintained a teacher-student ratio of 1:15, and sent about 90 per cent of its graduates to college. This high level of educational quality had been historically maintained and expected by the residents with virtually no trace of controversy.

Governance by consensus was an established and fundamental characteristic of the communities' political system. Both the municipal and school government were "organized so as to avoid social conflict and achieve administrative efficiency." In both instances the non-partisan, caucus method of nomination and election was used to tap public-minded citizens willing to rely on professional administrators to make major policy decisions and run the government on a day-to-day basis. In describing the political culture of these suburbs, Masotti writes:

> Nonpartisanship and conflict avoidance are the common themes; technical authority (represented by professional administrators) and the caucus system are the common mechanisms. . . . Controversy over public policy and partisan competition for public office are seen as a threat to the 'good life' and are resented as a disruption. . . . One of the major functions of the professional administrator in these communities is to contain or suppress social conflict; his job may depend on his ability to do this.[26]

For a period of 63 years, school government was successfully conducted in this manner. The citizens overwhelmingly approved every

---

[24] Louis M. Masotti, *Education and Politics in Suburbia: The New Trier Experience* (Cleveland: Press of Western Reserve University, 1967).

[25] *Ibid.*, p. 17.

[26] *Ibid.*, pp. 26-34.

bond referendum proposed, and were never confronted with a contested school board election. In the late 1950's and early 1960's, however, the long-time community-wide consensus on school matters dissolved over the issue of expanding school facilities. Between 1957 and 1961, two major referenda for building a second high school in the district were defeated, and public confidence in the school's decision-makers became unprecedently low. A large number of critical newspaper letters, hostile public statements, overt campaigns against board propositions, and heated board meetings characterized the period. This level of dissension was not reduced until the school board members and key administrators realized that they needed to reexamine their policies in light of community changes, and to engage in a professional public relations program to win back the community's trust and approval.

What happened to bring about what Masotti refers to as the "disintegration of the community" over school matters? He identifies two basic factors. First, while the population of the district had historically grown slowly (only 3 per cent between 1940 and 1950, for example), it experienced an increase of 42.3 per cent during the 1950's. In addition to swelling school enrollment, the unusual population growth created increased social differentiation within the district. Most of the newcomers were forced to concentrate in the western section of the district, which was less densely populated. Although the newcomers were as highly educated as the eastern residents, they were somewhat less wealthy, and were employed in less prestigious occupations. Also, a large number were eastern European Jews; "they were thus differentiated not only from the district's predominantly Protestant population, but also from the wealthier and more socially acceptable (in New Trier) German Jews in Glencoe."[27] The population growth and social differentiation, then, tended to establish an east-west dichotomy in the community which entailed four dimensions—native–newcomer, wealthy–less wealthy, Jew–Protestant, and eastern European Jew–German Jew.

Massotti argues that these differences were latent until the Board of Education proposed to build a second high school in the western section of the district. Then the factions became real.

> The 'natives' saw the Board's proposal as an opportunity to give the newer arrivals, whose migration to the community, they felt, had caused school overcrowding, 'a school of their own,' and at the same time relieve the pressure on old New Trier. The newcomers, on the other hand, saw it as an attempt by the Board of Education, biased in

---

[27] *Ibid.*, p. 126.

favor of the older residents, to provide 'separate but equal' facilities and thereby segregate them from the community they had worked so hard to join."[28]

The second major factor contributing to the emergence of conflict was the failure on the part of the board members to recognize the extent of social changes that had occurred in the community, or to realize that these changes necessitated an alteration in the decision-making procedures which had been so successful in the past. Not only did the board members underestimate the extent of enrollment growth until a crisis situation had occurred, but their proposals for dealing with the situation were insensitive to community opinion. The board was accustomed first to making policy decisions, after consultation with the administration, and then informing the community as to what was to be done. In the past this process was effective because of the high degree of consensus among the long-time residents of the community; however, it was not effective once a large number of newcomers with slightly divergent social characteristics migrated into the community. This was particularly so when the board's proposal would have, in effect, separated the newcomers from the established residents.

The New Trier School District eventually achieved reintegration, but not until the citizens and school decision-makers underwent a period of relatively serious dissension which emanated from social changes induced by postwar suburbanization. This case suggests that even in a relatively homogeneous suburban community, with a long history of harmony on school matters and with developed mechanisms to stifle conflict, the metropolitan process introduces sufficient demographic and social changes to increase the possibilities of community conflict over the education function.

IV. School District Reorganization

The rapid multiplication of suburban communities and rising school budgets have generated in some metropolitan areas a movement to consolidate several school districts. The proponents of consolidation usually stress several arguments to bolster their position. In the St. Louis metropolitan area, for example, the supporters of consolidation pointed out that the city school system had a 1966 enrollment of 116,000, one school board consisting of 12 members, one school superintendent, and one supporting administrative staff. In contrast, the St. Louis suburban ring, with a school enrollment of about 163,000, had

---

[28] *Ibid.*, pp. 127-28.

26 different boards of education with 164 members, 26 superintendents, and 26 administrative staffs. Further, school taxes in the suburbs ranged from $2.72 per $100 in affluent Clayton to $4.23 per $100 in the economically depressed community of Kinlock.[29]

Attacking the situation as uneconomical, inefficient, and inequitable, the backers of reorganization claimed that consolidation would reduce spiraling school costs because a single school district (or fewer districts) would have greater purchasing power, could take advantage of economics of scale, and could reduce duplication ranging all the way from superintendents to specialized teachers and equipment. Consolidation would also, according to the proponents, equalize the distribution of tax revenue throughout the entire suburban area so that all students would benefit from the tax base instead of only those who resided in suburbs with a substantial industrial and/or commercial base. A larger school system would supposedly also provide students currently in smaller systems with access to a more varied and comprehensive educational program.

Despite the apparent persuasiveness of these arguments, particularly from the perspective of suburbanites experiencing financial strain, there have been few instances in which suburban school systems have been reorganized into a larger unit. Resistance to reorganization rests on several grounds. Opponents argue that consolidation threatens community identity and endangers the close rapport between parents and school officials which supposedly exists in small districts. Consolidation also, of course, threatens the status of school administrators, office holders, and non-academics employees as well as educational specialists. Quite often, such groups will form the core of opposition to any reorganization effort. The residents of affluent suburbs also generally oppose consolidation because it would entail utilizing their tax base to help support less wealthy school systems in the suburban area. The combination of all these factors has constituted a significant barrier to suburban school consolidation. Consequently, although many commentators have suggested reorganization as a means for relieving suburbanites of rising educational costs, it appears that political resistance to such a change is very strong.[30]

The opposition to consolidation is even more intense if the proposal includes merging suburban school districts with the central city district.

---

[29] *St. Louis Post-Dispatch*, July 11, 1966.

[30] For an analysis of public attitudes in six metropolitan areas concerning consolidating suburban districts with each other, see: Basil G. Zimmer and Amos H. Hawley, *Metropolitan Area Schools: Resistance to District Reorganization* (Beverly Hills, California: Sage Publications Inc., 1968), pp. 161-163.

A recent study of six metropolitan areas found that, while almost a majority of central city residents favored such a plan, less than one-third of the suburbanites would vote for consolidation.[31] Indeed, almost a majority (48 per cent) of the suburban respondents in the largest metropolitan areas indicated that they would rather pay higher taxes to their present school system than lower taxes to a larger district which would include the central city.[32]

Given the fact that many suburbanites left the central city to escape its general atmosphere, it is quite understandable that many would be opposed to a measure that would governmentally reunite them with the city.[33] In fact, it is likely that this resistance to consolidate with the core city has become even firmer with the eruption of racial tension and violence in recent years. One must also recall that many city migrants selected a particular suburb because of the quality of its school system, and that the gap between suburban and city schools has continuously widened. When all of these factors are taken into consideration, it becomes apparent that suburban and city school systems will remain separated for the foreseeable future.

V. School Integration in Suburbia

The infeasibility of merging suburban and city school systems involves not only economic implications, but also important social implications. As we noted earlier, the metropolitan process has operated as a sorting mechanism which has and continues to separate school populations by race. Thousands of suburban schools are populated by virtually all-white student bodies, while city schools are increasingly composed of black students. The declining proportion of white students in city schools and the almost total absence of black students in suburban schools means that the degree of *de facto* school segregation in the North will become greater. Many commentators point to Washington D.C., where it is impossible to achieve integrated education because 92 per cent of the student population is black, as the pattern for other large cities in the future.

---

[31] *Ibid.*, pp. 155-161.

[32] *Ibid.*, pp. 167-174.

[33] Concerning the general suburban resistance to reorganization see: Advisory Commission on Intergovernmental Relations, *Factors Affecting Voter Reactions to Governmental Reorganization in Metropolitan Areas* (Washington, D.C.: U.S. Government Printing Office, 1962); Scott Greer, *Metropolitics* (New York: John Wiley and Sons, 1963); Roscoe C. Martin, *Metropolis in Transition* (Washington, D.C.: U.S. Government Printing Office, 1963).

The growing concentration of white students in suburbs and black students in cities constitutes an extremely disturbing trend for those who maintain that integrated education is a desirable goal. Such a concentration pattern means that integration is not possible without some sort of city-suburban merger. Integration proponents, as discussed in the following chapter, have failed to attain integration within city school systems because of a variety of political barriers. The existence of school district boundaries adds a seemingly insurmountable obstacle in the quest for school integration. Consequently, given the general population trends and the general resistance to city-suburban consolidation, it is doubtful that proponents of school integration will have any more success in the future than they have had in the past. Suburbanites seem to be just as resistant to the changes necessary for obtaining integration as have been city residents.

The nature of suburban resistance to alterations that would implement integrated education is illustrated by a 1969 event in the suburb of Great Neck, New York. Great Neck is a residential suburb of 50,000, populated primarily by Jewish migrants from New York City who are college-educated, hold professional and white collar jobs, and have high incomes.[34] The community had a 1968 school population of about 10,000 students, including 400 black students. In 1968, the Center for Urban Education, a private educational organization located in New York City, recommended to the community a busing program that would improve the social understanding of suburban pupils and stimulate academic achievement among black and Puerto Rican students. The proposal called for transporting 45 to 60 central city pupils into the primary grades of the Great Neck school system. During the first year of the plan, the pupils would be placed by pairs in classes not exceeding 22 children. In the second year, the students would be placed only in kindergarten, and at the end of the second year the program would be evaluated to determine whether or not it should continue.

After the proposal was presented, the Great Neck School Board decided, against the advice of State Education Commissioner, James E. Allen Jr. (who reminded the board members that the responsibility for the decision was theirs) to conduct a public referendum on the issue, and pledged to abide by the majority vote. Although a large majority of community organizations supported the plan, vigorous opposition was provided by the Parents Committee Against New York

---

[34] *New York Times*, February 8, 1969, and *Newsweek* (February 17, 1969), pp. 69-70.

City-Great Neck School Busing. Through a newspaper and telephone canvassing campaign, the opponents of the proposal argued that it might lead to higher school taxes (the program would be supported by outside funds), and that the racial hostilities aroused in New York City over school decentralization might spill over into Great Neck. As a result, the proposal was defeated in the referendum by a vote of 5,797 to 4,988. In an emotionally charged meeting following the referendum, the school board voted 3-2 to proceed with the plan despite the voting results. This action, of course, sparked a serious community conflict over the schools which continues today.

The broader implications of the Great Neck incident for school integration in the North was perhaps best summarized by Viron Jones, director of the Great Neck National Association for the Advancement of Colored People, who remarked during the controversy: "After all, if liberal Great Neck won't accept 60 little black children in its schools, can you really expect that anybody else will?"[35]

If integrated education continues to be pursued as a goal, many other suburban communities will be confronted with the issue, and their response may well determine whether or not integration will be realized. Thus far, proponents of integration are not optimistic. There is considerable suburban resistance to consolidation and token integration programs, and there are also indications that many suburbanites will strongly resist eliminating *de facto* segregation within their own community. This point is supported by the case of Teaneck, New Jersey, which illustrates the intensity of white resistance to integration even in suburban communities where the socio-economic disparity between the races is relatively small.[36]

Teaneck is a prosperous, upper-middle class, residential suburb. During the 1930's and 1940's a black neighborhood developed in adjacent Englewood which bordered on Teaneck. Officials in Teaneck responded with discussions of various ways to keep blacks out of the community, and convinced the state to build a highway along the border and erect a high fence. When a black family did purchase a home, a cross was burned on their lawn and their school children were stoned. They left the community within a few weeks. During the 1950's, Teaneck experienced the process caused by a black family that did stay: the panic selling among neighboring white homeowners, the "block busting" techniques of real estate agents, the creation of an organization to counter panic selling, and the reluctant relegation of a

---

[35] Quoted in *Newsweek* (February 17, 1969), p. 70.
[36] See Reginald G. Damerell, *Triumph in a White Suburb* (New York: William Morrow & Company, Inc., 1968).

section of the suburb to blacks. The informal restriction of blacks to a particular residential section of the community created, of course, *de facto* segregation in the school system. Although blacks constituted only 4 per cent of the community's population in 1961, black pupils exceeded 30 per cent of the population in two elementary schools. By 1963 these proportions increased to 50 per cent in one school and almost 40 per cent in the other, despite introduction of a volunteer open-enrollment plan established by the board of education. The failure of the open-enrollment plan convinced the superintendent of schools that he must persuade the board members to institute a mandatory integration program that would eliminate segregation.

Although the black students were overwhelmingly middle-class in their characteristics, and 65 per cent of them went on to higher education, stiff opposition developed within the community against busing the black students to formerly all-white elementary schools. Only after many long and heated board meetings, numerous community debates, and a bitter school board election campaign resulting in a vote of confidence for the proponents of integration, did the school system institute an integration program. As the author of a recent study put it: "The awful truth is that integration in Teaneck *almost did not happen*. Only the most extraordinary confluence of favorable circumstances brought it about . . ."[37]

That integration came so painfully to Teaneck, where black students constituted only a small proportion of the school population and came from middle class families, suggests at least two conclusions. One, that there is much deep-seated white resistance toward even middle-class blacks. And second, the issue of integration is likely to generate school conflict even in suburban communities which appear to contain a largely white "liberal" population. Indeed, one might even suggest that the issue of integration will rival the level of school expenditures as the primary source of suburban school controversy in the near future.

VI. Summary

This chapter has illustrated some of the major impacts of metropolitanization on the operation of schools in suburbia. We noted that suburban schools, by virtue of their importance in the value structure of the population and the proportion of public revenues they receive, stand at the very center of suburban government. It was also pointed

---

[37] *Ibid.*, p. 348.

out, however, that a variety of mechanisms have been devised to isolate school governance from the political arena and to suppress public conflict over school matters.

Several case studies illustrated why these objectives have not been wholly successful, even in the type of suburban community referred to as "high status-low conflict."[38] We suggested that an important source of school conflict was the rapid growth of suburban school population coupled with population diversification and conflicting public attitudes on school expenditure levels. The controversies arising out of these factors were quite often intensified by the fact that few suburban educational decision-makers fully recognized the significance of the social changes which had been introduced into their communities.

Although school consolidation has been suggested as a mean for relieving the fiscal pressure on many suburbanites, there is considerable opposition to such a change. This resistance is particularly strong if a merger is to include the central city school system. The opposition to consolidation also carries implications for the proponents of achieving integrated education in the metropolitan North. As the white flight to the suburbs continues, the chances for integrating city schools decreases to the point where city-suburban consolidation becomes necessary. However, white suburban residents have not displayed any greater commitment to integrated education than white city dwellers.

The experience of suburban districts during the 1950's and 1960's provides clues to the future of urban education. While the rapid population growth of the last two decades may not be repeated during the next decade, suburban school population will continue to grow and the level of school expenditures will continue to be a major controversial issue. Two developments will probably add further fuel to this issue. On the one hand, there will be a growing number of whites with working class or lower middle class backgrounds who will flee the core cities and migrate to suburbia. These newcomers will join other suburbanites in resisting high education expenditures. Second, suburban communities will be pressed to devote larger sums of money to non-educational public services. As a consequence, school systems will find it increasingly difficult to command the high proportion of tax revenue that they have in the past.

The combination of these factors will tend to increase the "tax strain" on many suburbanites, stimulating them to be particularly

---

[38] David Minar, "The Community Basis of Conflict in School System Politics," *American Sociological Review* (December, 1966), pp. 822-35.

resistant to educational relationships with central city districts (such as consolidation or special integration programs) which might increase their taxes even more. These fiscal considerations and the growing hostility between the races will contribute to further suburban-city separation. Most suburban communities will tend to concentrate on securing sufficient resources to support a school system which will continue to send a large majority of suburban pupils into well-paying jobs or on to higher education, rather than contributing to the alleviation of central city educational problems.

School Politics in the City

4

I. Introduction

While the cluster of changes comprising metropolitanization stimulated a variety of problems in suburban school systems, these changes have had even greater consequences for city school systems. We noted earlier that suburban districts have sustained a rapid influx of new students; however, it is important to note that most of these students are from intact, middle-class families, which generally provide home settings conducive to educational stimulation and attainment. Consequently, the great majority of suburban students graduate from high school and large numbers go on to college. Although many suburban districts lack fortified tax bases to meet the needs of a fast-growing school population, the communities contain families which usually have steady and reasonably high incomes. Further, the continuous decentralization of economic activities from the core city outward promises some fiscal relief for portions of the suburban ring.[1]

It is much more difficult, if not impossible, to identify optimistic features of the impact of metropolitanism on city schools. The redistribution of people and economic activities has concentrated in city

---

[1] Dorothy K. Newman, "The Decentralization of Jobs," *Monthly Labor Review* (May, 1967), pp. 7-13.

schools a rapidly growing number of students from low-income black families, who require new and more costly educational efforts by the school system at the same time that the city's fiscal foundation is being eroded by the flight to the suburbs.

A mass of evidence indicates that the public school system has generally failed to adjust to these changing conditions. The Coleman Report found, for example, that Negro students in the metropolitan Northeast scored somewhat below white students on standard achievement tests at the first grade level, were about 1.6 grades behind by the sixth grade, 2.4 years behind by the ninth grade, and had fallen 3.3 grades behind white students by the twelfth grade. In assessing the performance of the school system, the report stated:

> For most minority groups, then, and most particularly the Negro, schools provide no opportunity at all for them to overcome this initial deficiency; in fact, they fall farther behind the white majority in the development of several skills which are critical to making a living and participating fully in modern society. Whatever may be the combination of nonschool factors—poverty, community attitudes, low educational level of parents—which put minority children at a disadvantage in verbal and non-verbal skills when they enter the first grade, the fact is the schools have not overcome it.[2]

One of the important results of this situation is that a greater proportion of black students than white students drop out of school. The Coleman Report found that, in the metropolitan North and West, black students were more than three times as likely to drop out of school than white students (20 per cent compared to 6 per cent). Those students who have graduated from ghetto schools also find it extremely difficult, because of the inferior education they have received, to secure decent-paying jobs or to be accepted by institutions of higher education.

The failure of the school system to provide black students with an adequate education was identified by the Kerner Commission Report as "one of the persistent sources of grievance and resentment within the Negro community."[3] The Report also noted that the hostility of both black parents and students toward the school system was a contributing factor to racial conflict within many city school districts, and to the outbreak of general civil disorders in American cities. Indeed, a

[2] *Equality of Educational Opportunity* (Washington, D.C.: U.S. Office of Education, U.S. Government Printing Office, 1966), p. 20.

[3] *Report of the National Advisory Commission on Civil Disorders* (New York: Bantam Books, 1968), p. 425.

recent survey concerning the eruption of civil disorders between January and March, 1968, concluded that "the overwhelming number of recorded disorders through March has centered around schools."[4]

These factors have placed city school systems in an environmental setting which makes it more difficult for the core decision-makers (the superintendent and board members) to monopolize the educational decisional process and to insulate themselves and the schools from political conflict. In fact, during the last few years, some city school systems have had their very existence threatened. To gain some understanding of why this situation has evolved, this chapter focuses on three developments of the 1960's which have contributed to the bulk of recent school controversies: (1) the civil rights struggle over school desegregation; (2) the unionization and growing militancy of teachers; and (3) the quest for community control of schools.

II. The Politics of Northern School Desegregation

Although it is difficult to pinpoint the exact beginnings of the current city school crisis, it is clear that the fight over *de facto* segregation in Northern schools was the opening wedge. Prior to 1954, Negro organizations had occasionally lodged protests against the informal segregation of the races in many Northern school districts, but rarely had the issue gained much attention. However, following the milestone Supreme Court decision of *Brown v. Topeka* (1954), which struck down the legality of the "separate but equal" educational systems in the South, renewed and intensified demands were also made against Northern *de facto* school segregation. A coalition of blacks and white liberals in numerous cities attempted to alter the school attendance patterns which had developed over the years as a result of segregated housing patterns and, in some cases, the gerrymandering of boundaries by school officials.[5] This section focuses on why these demands were made, who made them, how school officials reacted to the demands, and what factors appeared to influence the outcome of the political controversy surrounding this issue.

The exact conditions which stimulated the demand for Northern desegregation varied, of course, from city to city. The general pattern,

---

[4] Lemberg Center for the Study of Violence, Brandeis University, "Riot Data Review" (May, 1968), p. 30.

[5] For an illustrative case study of gerrymandering see: John Kaplan, "Segregation Litigation and the Schools-Part III: The Gary Litigation," *Northwestern University Law Review* (May-June, 1964), pp. 10-70.

however, was one in which a group of citizens (no doubt stimulated by the 1954 *Brown* decision) became seriously disturbed over two circumstances. First, that a large percentage of black students attended schools which were predominantly populated by blacks. Second, that the large proportion of black students were attending schools which were inferior in many respects to schools attended by most whites.[6]

Citizen groups in several cities produced reports documenting the differences. In general, the findings illustrated that "Negro" schools as contrasted to "white" schools were older, more run down, highly overcrowded, contained less special equipment, provided fewer special educational services and programs, had larger classes, and perhaps most importantly, were staffed by less experienced teachers, many of whom were daily substitutes. Combined with the family background and neighborhood environment of the students, the obvious end result of these in-school factors was inferior education for black students. Indeed, as was noted earlier, the most comprehensive national study of the educational disparities between whites and Negroes established that the longer Negro students remain in school, the further and further they fall behind white students in terms of standardized test scores which measure skills involved in attaining a good job in an increasingly technical society.[7]

Not trusting that substantially all-black schools would or could be upgraded to the point where black students would receive equal educational opportunities, the proponents of integration demanded that school officials take the necessary measures to create racially balanced schools, or, as was the case in some cities, protect the few schools that were integrated.[8] The supporters of integration argued that such measures would benefit black students, would have no adverse effects on white students, and would, in fact, better prepare them to live in a multi-racial society.

---

[6] A vivid description of such schools is contained in Jonathan Kozol, *Death at an Early Age* (New York: Bantam Books, 1967).

[7] The extent of school segregation in the United States, the differences between predominantly white and predominantly black schools, and the educational attainment gap between the races is thoroughly discussed in two major studies: *Equality of Educational Opportunity, op. cit.*, and United States Commission on Civil Rights, *Racial Isolation in the Public Schools* (Washington, D.C.: U.S. Government Printing Office, 1967).

[8] Robert L. Crain in *The Politics of School Desegregation* (Chicago: Aldine Publishing Company, 1968), pp. 106-117, points out that in four of the eight Northern cities he studied, interracial neighborhood groups and white liberals lead the desegregation fights in efforts to save integrated neighborhoods and schools from becoming all Negro.

Depending upon the nature of the *de facto* segregation situation in each city, one or more of the following mechanisms for achieving integration was suggested:

1. *Open enrollment*—Under this procedure students would be allowed to transfer from segregated or overcrowded schools to other schools in the system. Transportation would be provided by the school system.

2. *The Princeton Plan*—This mechanism would achieve integration by pairing adjacent "white" and "black" schools through a reallocation of students and grade levels to each school. Thus, one school would contain all of the students from both of the schools for grades 1-3 and the other would contain grades 4-6 for both student bodies.

3. *Revised site selection*—This practice called for building new schools only on sites that would encourage integration. A moratorium would be placed on construction of schools inside black ghettos and some students would be transported outside their immediate neighborhoods to attend the new schools.

4. *Rezoning of attendance areas*—This procedure entails the comprehensive redrawing of attendance lines and large-scale busing of students out of neighborhood schools. Some plans call for busing only black students, others include students of both races.

5. *Educational parks*—The development of educational parks involves abandoning neighborhood schools and establishing campus-like institutions which would serve, in some cases, students from the Head Start level through the junior college level. Thus, students would be drawn from greatly enlarged attendance areas (middle-sized cities might have a single educational park attended by all students) and would be distributed among smaller units within the park without regard to their race or the location of their neighborhoods.

6. *City-suburban consolidation*—Some proponents of integration recognize that integration will not be feasible in some large cities in the near future because of prevailing population trends. Consequently, they have called for consolidation of central city

and suburban school districts as the only viable means for achieving racially balanced schools.

Many mixtures and variations of the above mechanisms were included in the desegregation dialogue, but the significant point is that while there was much discussion of how to integrate schools, not a single large city successfully integrated its school system or reversed the trend toward greater segregation, although a limited number of black students were bused into formerly white schools in several cities. In fact, with the exception of a few middle-sized cities such as Berkeley, California and Evanston, Illinois, virtually all large northern city school systems were more segregated in 1967 than they were when the Supreme Court made its historic 1954 ruling.[9]

Population trends and technical difficulties hindered the proponents of integration from reversing this trend toward segregation; however, political obstacles proved to be the most important factors in the failure to achieve school integration. Beginning at the most fundamental level, integration advocates in many cities were unable even to persuade school officials to recognize *de facto* segregation as a policy problem. Quite often, school superintendents and board members responded initially by assuming a posture of "color-blindness." That is, they argued that it was improper and in some instances illegal for the school system to apply race as a criterion for assigning students (and in some cities, teachers) to schools, since such action could be considered discriminatory. Some school systems refused to take racial censuses on these grounds. It was frequently maintained that racial integration was a so-called "social problem," not an educational concern; consequently, the schools should not become involved in the issue. Crain found that adoption of this posture by school superintendents in response to the demand for integration was also characterized by "extreme defensiveness about the schools, coupled with an intolerance of 'lay' criticism."[10]

Integrationists, then, were confronted with the rudimentary task of convincing those individuals at the core of the educational decision-making process that the school hierarchy must recognize the existence

---

[9] U.S. Commission on Civil Rights, *op. cit.*, pp. 1-15. For a discussion of the Berkeley and Evanston programs see: "Affirmative Integration: Studies to Overcome *De Facto* Segregation in Public Schools," *Law and Society Review* (November, 1967), pp. 15-31, and Thomas D. Wagaman, "Desegregation in Berkeley: Some Applicable Lessons," *The Urban Review* (April, 1969), pp. 13-17.

[10] Crain, *op. cit.*, pp. 115-124.

of segregated education and had the responsibility of eradicating it. Through various tactics, including public disclosure of educational disparities, demonstrations, and boycotts, advocates of integration generally succeeded in persuading school officials at least to recognize the issue as legitimate, and in many cases to make policy statements in favor of integration. Attaining actual changes in the student composition of schools, however, was quite a different matter.

An analysis by Rogers of the efforts to desegregate New York City schools illustrates the gulf between such policy statements and the actual implementation of specific integration programs. He points out that:

> Some of the most 'advanced' policy statements ever written on school desegregation (going back as far as 1954 when it was not yet 'fashionable,' at least in the North) were advanced by New York City's Board of Education. And they recommended basic, not diversionary strategies, e.g., site selection, changes in feeder patterns, rezoning, and establishing educational complexes and parks. Yet, after more than a decade of such policy statements, there has been little implementation.[11]

Several factors intervened between policy statements endorsing integration and the realization of integrated school systems. Although the mixture of such factors varied from city to city, some key variables existed in numerous cases.

One of these factors has already been referred to: large city school superintendents did not generally take strong pro-integration positions. Many took rather ambivalent *status quo* positions on the issue and some, such as Benjamin C. Willis, who was the superintendent of Chicago schools until 1967, argued that integration efforts might have detrimental educational results.[12] Whether this behavior on the part of superintendents arose from their social backgrounds (as suggested by Crain) or from an unwillingness to press for change because it might threaten their positions of authority (as suggested by Dentler), the important point is that few leading educational experts, whom the

---

[11] David Rogers, "Obstacles to School Desegregation in New York City: A Benchmark Case" in Marilyn Gittell (ed.), *Educating an Urban Population* (Beverly Hills, California: Sage Publications, Inc., 1967), pp. 155-184. Also see his volume *110 Livingston Street: Politics and Bureaucracy in the New York City School System* (New York: Random House, 1968).

[12] For a discussion of Willis's position see: Marcia Lane Vespa, "Chicago Regional School Plans," *Integrated Education* (Oct.-Nov. 1963), p. 25, and John E. Coons, "Chicago," in *Law and Society, op. cit.*, pp. 80-88.

lay board members looked to for guidance, strongly advocated integration as an important educational goal.[13]

Certainly a key consideration supporting this stance was the superintendents' realization that any meaningful integration plan in large cities would necessitate busing students, thereby threatening the "neighborhood school" concept. In this sense, desegregation ran counter to educational doctrine, since professional educators had long stressed the merits of neighborhood schools as an antidote to the impersonality, weakening of primary groups, and general *anomie* which supposedly characterizes urban life. In an effort to make the school a countervailing force in such an environment, educators advocated such reenforcing policies as building schools within residential areas, zoning to minimize student travel, gerrymandering boundary lines to preserve ethnic and class homogeneity, and constructing small schools. Implementation of these policies preserved the neighborhood school as a viable unit. Indeed, one might argue that schoolmen were so successful in selling the benefits of neighborhood schools and in centering activities around them, that they became captives of the concept, and not only provided opponents of integration with a slogan—"save our neighborhood schools"—but provided one that was bolstered by established educational philosophy and practice. Of course, few educators or opponents of integration noted that the neighborhood school concept had been repeatedly violated in numerous cities in order to concentrate black students in selected schools.[14]

The groups which typically rallied around the neighborhood school notion, forming a loose coalition, included professional groups inside the school system, local parent associations, home-owner groups, some civic organizations, and some real estate associations. These groups were bolstered by a constituency which has been described in the following manner:

> They represent lower-and lower-middle class populations recently migrated from central city slums and decaying areas. They want to keep their new neighborhood 'respectable' by preserving uncrowded,

---

13 Crain, *op. cit.*, pp. 115-124, suggests that superintendents generally derive from lower socio-economic backgrounds than their positions would suggest and thus feel insecure, which motivates them to act defensively toward any criticism or suggested change. Dentler stresses their unwillingness to jeopardize their authority within the school bureaucracy over a highly controversial issue on which they may lose. See: Robert Dentler, "Barriers to Northern School Desegregation" in Talcott Parsons and Kenneth C. Clark (eds.), *The Negro American* (Boston: Beacon Press, 1966), pp. 55-57.

14 Meyer Weinberg, *Race and Place: A Legal History of the Neighborhood School* (Washington, D.C.: U.S. Office of Education, U.S. Government Printing Office, 1967).

'good' schools and safe living conditions. They are an ethnocentric and highly status-conscious second generation, proud of the way they rose from a proletarian existence through their own efforts. They say that if the Negro had any ambition, he could do the same. Many of these whites are home-owners anxious about declining property values if Negroes move into their area. As parents, they are concerned about the upward mobility and occupational achievement of their children which they see as threatened by forced desegregation and, they reason, a decline in quality of education.[15]

In the above description, it is particularly important to note the stress placed on the attitude of preserving "respectable" neighborhoods. This emphasis suggests that the desire to preserve neighborhood schools is not wholly an educational consideration, but is intimately interrelated to the preservation of neighborhoods. Other scholars have also stressed this point. In an analysis of the school desegregation conflict in Boston, the researchers concluded that the school fight represented "something much deeper and more meaningful for our times—*the perception of a threat to familiar, secure, and comfortable ways.* The hard resistance to this perceived threat has formed not around school segregation, which is an outpost, but around neighborhood segregation, which is the inner citadel. In the magic words 'neighborhood schools,' the emphasis is on the first, not the second word."[16]

Viewed in this context, it is apparent why numerous local groups have so vehemently resisted school desegregation efforts. Many of their members did not particularly object to their children's attending integrated schools (as long as white students were a substantial majority), but they did object to forced school alterations which they considered the first step in changing the character of their neighborhoods. Consequently, the proponents of integration were faced with a powerful, though perhaps unplanned, coalition of white citizens who viewed most desegregation plans as a threat to their children's education, their homes, and their neighborhoods, and of professional educators who had long espoused the values of neighborhood schools, around which many had built their careers.

Integration proponents were generally unsuccessful in fashioning a coalition to match the strength of the opposition. They were usually outnumbered and often weakened by internal cleavages. In some

---

[15] Rogers, "Obstacles to School Desegregation in New York City," pp. 165-166. Rogers has also pointed out that neighborhood school advocates resent "the fact that upper middle class 'white liberals' have placed them on the firing line while sending their own children to private schools or while planning to move out." *110 Livingston Street*, p. 80.

[16] J. Michael Ross, Thomas Crawford, Thomas Pettigrew, "Negro Neighbors—Banned in Boston," *Trans-Action* (September-October, 1966), pp. 13-18.

instances they split over goals, with some factions willing to settle, at least initially, for symbolic goals (i.e., policy statements), while other factions were determined to push for concrete results, i.e., a certain number of schools actually desegregated. Disunity also developed over tactics, leadership struggles, and the pace of change.[17] Commenting on the inability of civil rights organizations and "white liberal" groups to operate cohesively on the issue, Rogers states that:

> These groups have rarely been solidly united on any school desegregation issue for any extended time. Divergent loyalties, status affiliation, leadership clashes, organizational imperatives, and constituent pressures have quite consistently prevented much united action except in periods of extreme crisis or extreme clarity as to the board's intentions and actions.[18]

Besides fragmentation, integrationists in several cities were also confronted with the difficulty of building grass-roots support for their position. While some black parents were willing to have their children bused out of their neighborhoods, other expressed reservations about transferring their children into strange white neighborhoods and argued instead for the upgrading of their own schools. There is evidence to suggest that school personnel sometimes contributed to the development of such attitudes by not providing parents with accurate information about what was involved in various integration programs and how their children would be affected.[19] Some black militants also weakened grass-roots support for integration. Julius Hobson, the individual who filed a court suit which led to a 1967 ruling that found the Washington, D.C. schools guilty of discrimination, stated that he was opposed to busing until "something is done about the psychological ills" which exist in white communities.[20]

Whether greater cohesion and grass-roots support among integrationist would have materially increased the number of integrated schools in large cities is questionable. First, there is the point that

---

[17] Crain, *op. cit.*, pp. 21-22.

[18] "Obstacles to School Desegregation in New York City," p. 172. Also see Bert E. Swanson, *School Integration Controversies in New York* (Washington, D.C.: U.S. Office of Education, Cooperative Research Project No. 2857, 1965), p. 88, on this point.

[19] Rogers, *110 Livingston Street*, pp. 30-31.

[20] In a statement before the Education Writers' Association annual meeting, quoted in *Chicago Tribune*, February 18, 1968.

changing population composition of core cities makes it increasingly difficult to integrate schools because the number of available white students is steadily decreasing. Second, both major studies which compared results of the school integration conflict in several cities concluded tentatively that the intensity of proponent activities seemed to have only marginal effects on the behavior of school board members.[21] Board members tended to maintain whatever posture they had assumed early in the conflict, and that posture was largely determined by their attitudes toward the overall race issue rather than by the activity of school integration proponents. These basic attitudes did not generally encourage sweeping changes in school operation. The action taken by school boards in large cities reflects this fundamental posture, which, of course, was supported by the majority of white citizens.

In summary, then, the combination of strong opposition on the part of some educators, school board members, and white citizen groups, and internal difficulties within the integrationists' camp effectively prevented the realization of any meaningful integration program in large northern cities. The significance of the desegregation conflict, however, goes beyond the general outcome of the struggle. It can be argued that the controversy stimulated a wide variety of previously-uninvolved individuals to seek some influence in shaping educational policy. As a result of this new citizen involvement, schoolmen found that their desire to insulate the schools from political conflict and their claim to expertise on important school matters was seriously challenged. In other words, although the proponents of integration did not achieve their ultimate objective, the impact of their action contributed to a significant weakening of the protective wall which had surrounded the governance of city schools. Further, and perhaps more importantly, the failure to achieve integrated education convinced some proponents of change that the only way the quality of education for ghetto students could be improved would be to gain community control of the schools. Instead of exerting energy to convince the "white power structure" to alter its policy decisions, the emphasis shifted to devising means which would allow ghetto communities to make their own school policy decisions. This shift in focus, however, has stimulated considerable resistance from another group of actors who have recently sought to gain influence in educational policy-making. The quest for teacher power is the topic we turn to next.

---

[21] Crain, *op. cit.*, p. 138, and *Law and Society, op. cit.*, pp. 94-97.

III. Teachers Seek Power

Historically, teachers have played a very minor role in shaping educational policy.[22] Indeed, until the development of the human relations movement of the 1940's, prevailing educational doctrine virtually excluded teachers from even a consulting role. The chief school administrator was the dominant education figure with a monopoly on expertise. The role of the teacher was to implement the decisions made at the top.[23]

The human relations movement altered this pattern. Influenced by the research findings of industrial organizations, educational doctrine shifted to an emphasis on "internal democracy." Noting the difference between autocratic and democratic leadership, stress in educational circles was placed on involving teachers in the formulation of policy.[24] The rationale behind this shift was that teacher participation would improve staff performance and facilitate administration. If teachers were involved in working on a problem, shaping alternative approaches, and influencing the final course of action, it was reasoned that they would be more willing to cooperate in implementing the policy. This cooperative approach would presumably promote more effective administrative control by discouraging tendencies toward an anti-managerial orientation.

This notion of democracy contained an important qualifying dimension. Although teachers would be involved and consulted in educational policy-making, they had to recognize that the power for final decisions remained with the administrators, particularly with the school superintendent, insofar as the board had delegated responsibility to him. Until quite recently, teachers accepted this definition of the situation. The largest teacher's organization, the National Education Association, supported this posture via its inclusion of administrators in the organization and the prominent role of administrators in the hierarachy of the NEA.[25]

---

[22] The role has been so minor that a recent comprehensive analysis of educational literature does not even include a section on the role of teachers in policymaking. See: John F. Gallagher, *Decision Making in Public Education: Views from the Professional Literature* (University of California, Davis: Institute of Governmental Affairs, 1965).

[23] Alan Rosenthal, "Administrator-Teacher Relations: Harmony or Conflict?" *Public Administration Review* (June, 1967), pp. 154-161.

[24] An early statement of shift is contained in American Association of School Administrators, *Morale For a Free World* (Washington, D.C.: The Association, 1944), pp. 256-265.

[25] James D. Koerner, *Who Controls American Education?* (Boston: Beacon Press, 1968), p. 38.

Acquiescence to this situation on the part of teachers has been dramatically altered by the emergence of the American Federation of Teachers, an affiliate of the AFL-CIO. Although it was founded in 1916, the AFT was, for the most part, ineffective until its New York City local, the United Federation of Teachers, won the right to bargain for New York teachers in 1961, and then gained substantial benefits after threatening to strike in 1963. Since those two events, many teachers across the nation have taken militant action in an attempt to shape a new decision-making role for themselves. Discontent with the traditionally subordinate position of teachers has stimulated the rapid expansion and growth of teacher unions in New York, Baltimore, Boston, Cleveland, Detroit, Philadelphia, San Francisco, and Washington, D.C., and raised the cry for teachers to assume an equal status in the policy-making process.

The changing student composition of large city schools and the supposed decline in working conditions resulting from such changes appears to be a prime factor in the teachers' efforts to participate in policy-making. The relatively low monetary rewards accompanying such working conditions and the growing number of male teachers are also fundamental to the growth of unions and new teacher militancy.[26] The increasing bureaucratization of school systems and the subsequent bureaucratic strength of the administration has also stimulated teacher organization. Perhaps even more important is the UFT's demonstration to teachers throughout the nation that they could effectively utilize the strike tactic to win a showdown with the administration and board of education. The resulting new-found confidence has helped teachers to change their self image. In the words of Albert Shanker, president of the UFT, "the image of the good old dedicated teacher who gets kicked around and once a year, on Teacher Recognition Day, is handed a flower for his lapel," no longer applies.[27] This new self image stresses the potency and determination of teachers to take what they feel is their rightful role in running the schools.

---

[26] In one of the few empirical studies on this subject, it was found that not only are men more likely to join a teachers' union, but that female teachers in a "male climate" (a high proportion of male union members) are also likely to join a union. See: Alan Rosenthal "The Strength of Teacher Organizations: Factors Influencing Membership in Two Large Cities," *Sociology of Education* (Fall, 1966), pp. 359-380, and Alan Rosenthal, *Pedagogues and Power: Teacher Groups in School Politics* (Syracuse: Syracuse University Press, 1969), pp. 13-14.

[27] *New York Times*, January 12, 1968. Also see: Wesley A. Wildman, "What Prompts Greater Teacher Militancy?" *School Board Journal* (March, 1967), pp. 27-32, and Rollin B. Posey, "The New Militancy of Public Employees," *Public Administration Review* (March/April, 1968), pp. 111-117.

Also stimulating the new teacher militancy is the intensive rivalry which has recently sprung up between the NEA and the AFT. With a membership of over one million, the NEA has historically been the largest and most powerful teacher organization. It has stressed that it is a professional association, not a labor union, and has traditionally relied on "professionally accepted" means for improving educational standards for teachers and schools. In contrast, the AFT, with a membership of about 155,000 (concentrated in large cities and including teachers only), has operated in the tradition of the labor movement and has resorted, when necessary, to use of the strike to gain benefits for its membership. The rather remarkable victories achieved by the AFT during the 1960's have pushed the NEA toward a more militant position. More specifically, the NEA was still debating, in 1960, whether or not teacher negotiations with school boards was "compatible with the ethics and dignity of the teaching profession."[28] By the mid-1960's the NEA was promoting "professional negotiations," which it carefully distinquished from collective bargaining, and had settled on "professional sanctions" rather than the strike as a weapon. Sanctions include disaccreditation of a school system, urging teachers to boycott the system, and providing help for teachers in finding jobs elsewhere. The NEA levied statewide sanctions against Utah in 1964, Oklahoma in 1965, and Florida in 1967. Then in 1967 the NEA adopted a resolution at its national convention to support local chapters that felt it necessary to strike. Thus, by 1967, the policy of the NEA was difficult to distinquish from that of the AFT, and some commentators were predicting a merger of the two organizations.[29] As of 1969, such a merger had not occurred, and both organizations were using increasingly militant tactics to prove to their respective members that they could achieve teacher demands.

The growing number of teacher strikes is a good index of the general trend toward militancy. The Bureau of Labor Statistics reported only 35 teacher strikes in the decade 1955-1965. In the year 1966, however, there were 36 teacher strikes and numerous work stoppages. During 1967, there were more than 30 strikes in Michigan alone. And by 1968, the number of teacher strikes throughout the nation was over a hundred. All of this has occurred despite the fact that teacher strikes are illegal in the 50 states.

---

28 T. M. Stinnett, Jack H. Kleinmann, and Martha L. Ware, *Professional Negotiation in Public Education* (New York: Macmillan, 1966), p. 9.

29 Myron Liberman and Michael H. Moskow, *Collective Negotiations for Teachers, An Approach to School Administration* (Chicago: Rand McNally and Company, 1966), p. 403.

While early strikes generally concentrated on the salary issue, teacher organizations have recently included a wide variety of policy issues in their demand package. In the 1967 New York City strike, for example, the teachers not only called for increased salaries but for shorter working hours for some specialized school personnel, more preparation periods for teachers, expansion of special programs for disadvantaged students, the right to remove "disruptive" children from their classrooms, and reduction in class size. The 1968 strike in New York City centered around a controversial decentralization plan (discussed later in this chapter). Teachers are demanding not only higher pay and better working conditions, but involvement in virtually all phases of school policy-making.

Evidence suggests that this effort will become even stronger in the future. A study of the attitudes among leaders of teacher organizations in five large cities (Atlanta, Boston, Chicago, New York, and San Francisco) found strong agreement among the teacher leaders that the bulk of power over school policies was concentrated in the hands of board members, the superintendent, and the upper echelons of the central administration. The teachers considered themselves relatively powerless yet deserving of more power. With the exception of the leadership in Chicago, a majority of union leaders felt that teachers should have at least an equal voice in school decision-making.[30] And their actions in recent years imply that they are determined to acquire it.

The teachers' quest to carve out a new position for themselves has obviously had an important impact on the governance of schools, particularly in large cities with more militant teacher organizations. Teacher action has challenged the traditional domain of administrators and board members, and has introduced, in numerous cases, sufficient conflict to close down school systems. As a consequence, the entire prevailing power configuration in many school systems has altered and the educators' wish to project an image of consensus to the general public has been frustrated. In addition to breaching the non-conflict, apolitical norms of the education function, the development of teacher power has also endangered the principle of nonpartisanship. The more militant and successful organizations are usually affiliated with labor, which traditionally has been an important component of the Democratic Party coalition. Many educators find this development a serious threat to widespread public support of the schools. Public support is

---

[30] Alan Rosenthal, "Pedagogues and Power: A Descriptive Survey," *Urban Affairs Quarterly* (September, 1966), pp. 83-102.

also threatened by the belief that teacher victories will invariably result in expanded educational budgets. Given the fiscal conditions of the cities, it is apparent that growth of teacher bargaining power will intensify the fiscal difficulties facing city school districts.[31]

There are few indications that these trends will not continue. Teacher groups will increase their strength and will continue to broaden the scope of issues in which they demand an equal voice. This push by teachers and their willingness to utilize militant tactics will no doubt widen the cleavage between them and administrators. A new power alignment among teachers, administrators and the lay boards of education will probably result, and teachers will improve their position. Teacher organizations will contribute to the future conflict surrounding school government and will be an important wedge in breaking down the closed decision-making system which has characterized city school systems. Indeed, the position assumed by teacher groups may well be the determining factor in the future of city education, particularly in relationship to the issue of community control.

IV. The Quest for Community Control of Schools

The unsuccessful attempt to integrate education reflects the general failure of the civil rights movement to achieve its overall integration goals. Consequently, some black leaders and groups have introduced a fundamental shift in the goals and means for securing racial equality in America. Instead of pressing for acceptance into white society, the recent emphasis is on development of black independence and self-determination—the pursuit of black power—which *does not* mean reverse racism or the exploitation of whites by blacks. The term "black power" includes: development of a new self image among black people, with emphasis on racial pride (schools are very important in this respect); development of a sense of community and group cohesion; black control over black organizations; and black control or full participation in the decision-making processes of institutions which shape the lives of black people.[32]

In addition to the development of black power ideology, the push for community control of schools may also have been stimulated by the early emphasis on citizen participation in the anti-poverty program

---

[31] It is also possible that this development may, in the long run, actually decrease the fiscal burden at the local level by increasing greater state and federal contributions to education. More will be said along these lines in Chapters 5 and 6.

[32] Stokely Carmichael and Charles V. Hamilton, *Black Power: The Politics of Liberation* (New York: Vintage, 1967).

and the emergence of new leadership which grew out of that program. Although it is now clear that many federal officials and congressmen did not fully understand or support the concept of "maximum feasible participation" by those citizens affected by the poverty legislation, it is also clear that many citizens took the notion very seriously.[33] Consequently, the idea that low-income people should be intimately involved in the decision-making process of programs that influence their lives is becoming firmly accepted among ghetto residents.[34]

The most fundamental point emphasized by the proponents of community control is that the educational failure experienced by large numbers of students does not derive primarily from the characteristics of the ghetto students, but from the characteristics of the school system. They argue that the schools are geared to white, middle-class students and are run by white, middle-class professionals who have little understanding of or rapport with lower-income pupils. This lack of understanding is reflected, according to the critics, in the fact that educators utilize curriculum material which is irrelevant to ghetto children and rely on outmoded pedagogical practices that discourage rather than encourage children to learn. Some people argue that prevailing curriculum and pedagogical principles do not work even for white students, who achieve in spite of their schoolroom experience.[35]

Perhaps more important than curriculum material and teaching methods is the issue of teacher expectations. Many teachers in ghetto schools believe that low-income students cannot achieve at standard levels; thus, they have low expectations of student performance. The students sense this attitude, and for the most part fulfill the low expectations, so the teachers' attitudes operate as a self-fulfilling prophecy. A recent study indicates that this thesis may be a significant dimension of the urban education problem.[36] The authors of the study were

---

[33] For a discussion of the misunderstanding surrounding citizen participation see: John C. Donovan, *The Politics of Poverty* (New York: Pegasus, 1967), and Daniel P. Moynihan, *Maximum Feasible Misunderstanding* (New York: The Free Press, 1969).

[34] See, for example, the results of the poll reported in Gladys Engel, *Responses to a Decentralization Crisis* (New York: The Center for Urban Education, July, 1968).

[35] S. Alan Cohen, "Local Control and the Cultural Deprivation Fallacy," *Phi Delta Kappan* (January, 1969), pp. 255-259.

[36] Robert Rosenthal and Lenore Jacobson, *Pygmalion in the Classroom* (New York: Holt, Rinehart and Winston, Inc., 1968). Also see Edmund Gordon and Doxey Wilkerson, *Contemporary Education for the Disadvantaged* (New York: College Entrance Examination Board, 1966), pp. 56-57, for a discussion of the impact of teacher attitudes on the failure of compensatory education programs, and Herbert Kohl, *36 Children* (New York: New American Library, 1967) for an account of how "culturally deprived" children respond to a teacher with high expectations.

interested in testing the proposition that favorable expectations by teachers could lead to increased intellectual performance on the part of low-income pupils. The researchers administered a test to 200 children, which would attempt to predict the possibilities of intellectual "blooming." They then randomly selected 20 per cent of the children and informed their teachers that they were "potential bloomers," although the students were actually no different than the other students. After a year, the students identified as "bloomers" made significant gains compared to a control group, despite the fact that the only difference between the students was the mental image their teachers had of them. Although this study has been criticized on methodological grounds, its finding is supported by numerous observers of ghetto schools.

Critics also argue that city school systems have become "over-bureaucratized" to the point where energetic and innovative teachers simply give up, either by accepting the situation or by leaving the educational professional. Community control is looked upon as the most promising means for dismantling the ponderous bureaucratic structure.

Finally, supporters of community control also point out that professional educators have maintained a monopoly of control over ghetto schools but have failed, by any measures used, to produce positive results. Thus, greater participation by community residents could only improve the situation and, indeed, is a prerequisite for any meaningful innovation in school systems. Under a decentralized school system, innovation would be easier to achieve because the points of decision would be more visible and obstacles more readily identifiable. Further, greater community involvement would combat the alienation and distrust many ghetto parents and students harbor toward the schools, since the school would be more accountable to community residents.[37]

Although the degree of envisioned local control is often ambiguous, the proponents feel that community control can only be successful if there is *significant* community involvement in key policy decisions, particularly in the areas of personnel, curriculum, budget, and overall evaluation. This does not mean that parents and other community participants seek to run the schools themselves. It does mean that they want to be involved in key policy decisions and want to insure that the professionals working in the schools are responsive to the needs of the

[37] Marilyn Gittell, "Community Control of Education," in Robert H. Connery (ed.), *Urban Riots: Violence and Social Change* (New York: Columbia University, The Academy of Political Science, 1968), pp. 62-63.

community and its children. They want to create an environment in which educational innovation will be possible and welcome. If educational failure continues as the norm, they want the power to institute changes that will remedy the situation.[38]

The opponents of local control maintain that job security and the morale of the teaching force would be seriously jeopardized by community control. They fear that reallocation of power would undermine professional personnel standards and would result in a return to the patronage, corruption, and educational chaos that characterized many urban school systems earlier in the century. They feel that ethnic, religious, and ideological characteristics will be substituted for professional qualifications in the hiring and firing of teachers. Such a development would in turn compromise the objective teaching of material and thus reinforce the parochialism that education is designed to overcome. Opponents argue that parents and other community residents simply lack the qualifications for understanding the technical aspects of the educational process, and that greater involvement on their part would lead to a lower rather than higher quality of education.

Some opponents also affirm that decentralization would further decrease any possibilities of achieving integrated education and would contribute to the growing separation of the races in American society. It is intimated that the parochialism fostered in homogeneous local districts would encourage even greater racism among both whites and blacks. Such a development would have long-range detrimental effects on the resolution of society's race problem.

Finally, there is the charge that decentralizing large city school systems would increase the cost of education at a time when many systems are already under severe fiscal strain. Duplication of services would mean spending a greater proportion of funds on administration rather than on classroom personnel and materials.[39]

Whether community control will be achieved or whether the movement will suffer a fate similar to that of the integration movement is still unclear. As was the case with the integration issue, the encounter of the New York City school system with community control may well

---

[38] Robert A. Dentler, "For Local Control of the Schools," *Atlantic* (January, 1969), pp. 77-79.

[39] The main arguments against community control can be found in such articles as: John R. Everett, "The Decentralization Fiasco in our Ghetto Schools," *Atlantic* (December, 1968), pp. 71-73; Richard L. Featherstone and Frederick W. Hill, "Urban School Decentralization," *American School and University* (December, 1968), pp. 45-48; and *The United Federation of Teachers Looks at School Decentralization* (New York: United Federation of Teachers, 1968).

forecast the outcome of decentralization in other large cities. For this reason it is instructive to summarize and reflect upon the New York City experience.[40]

The thrust for community control in New York City was stimulated by the failure of the Board of Education to integrate a newly built intermediate school in East Harlem, I.S. 201.[41] During the school's construction, officials, including Superintendent Donovan, publicly assured parents that the new school would be integrated. In the spring of 1966, just before I.S. 201 was scheduled to open, however, the board announced that the student body would be composed of approximately 50 per cent Negro children and 50 per cent Puerto Rican children. The community was outraged at this definition of integration, and eventually decided that if they were going to be saddled with another segregated school they would attempt to run it themselves. After much parent agitation, including pressure to remove the white principal of the school, and assistance from the Ford Foundation, the Board of Education announced that it would set up several local districts "to experiment with varying forms of decentralization and community involvement." Thus, in 1967, the Board established the five-school I.S. 201 complex in Harlem, the eight-school Ocean Hill-Brownsville district in Brooklyn, and the five-school Two Bridges district in lower Manhattan as the experimental districts which would be "somewhat autonomous." Each district formed a governing board made up of parents, teachers, community representatives, school administrators, and university representatives. None of these groups, however, knew what "somewhat autonomous" meant, and despite several efforts by the governing boards to clarify the issue, the central Board never specified the powers delegated to the local boards of the experimental districts.

During the late summer of 1967, while planning the execution of the experiment, the teachers and community members of the local boards occasionally clashed. On September 2, 1967, the Ocean Hill-Brownsville

---

40 The literature on the New York City decentralization crisis is voluminous. The best starting point is the "Decentralization Bibliography" (New York: Center for Urban Education, 1968-1969). For contrasting views and interpretations see: Martin Mayer, *The Teachers Strike: New York, 1968* (New York: Harper and Row, 1969); Joseph Featherstone, "Community Control of Schools," *The New Republic* (March 29, 1969), pp. 19-22; New York Civil Liberties Union, *The Burden of Blame: A Report on the Ocean Hill-Brownsville School Controversy* (New York: Civil Liberties Union, October 9, 1968); Tom Brooks, "Tragedy at Ocean Hill," *Dissent* (January-February, 1969), pp. 28-40; Lillian S. Calhoun, "New York: Schools and Power—Whose?" *Integrated Education* (January-February, 1969), pp. 11-35; and Carol A. Wielk, *The Ocean Hill-Brownsville School Project: A Profile* (New York: Queens College, Institute for Community Studies, 1969).

41 See Rogers, *110 Livingston Street, op. cit.*, pp. 364-370.

board appointed five new principals to replace five incumbent principals who left the district at the start of the experiment. Some of the teachers became disturbed over the appointments because, although the new principals were well-qualified and all had state certification, they were not on the approved Civil Service list.[42] Relationships between community members and teachers deteriorated dramatically in the following weeks as a result of a city-wide strike called by the United Federation of Teachers. Among the union demands for pay increases, smaller classes, and expansion of a compensatory education program, was a clause to provide teachers with the right to exclude "disruptive children" from their classrooms. Many community members considered this a racist move on the part of the union, and attacked it bitterly. They also resented the fact that the union did not exempt the experimental districts from the strike, so they refused to support the striking teachers. A strong effort was made to keep the Ocean Hill schools open, and ugly clashes erupted on the picket lines.

Hostility between the teacher's union and the community was further intensified when the union teachers resigned from the local governing board and the U.F.T. joined the Council of Supervisory Associations in a lawsuit to oust the five new principals in Ocean Hill. Many teachers did not wish to return to Ocean Hill, and eighteen assistant principals resigned from the district in November. Parents accused the union of sabotage, and the teachers retaliated with charges against "black power," "militants" and "extremists."

During this same period, the New York State Legislature had advised Mayor John Lindsay to prepare a decentralization plan for the school system to increase its proportion of state educational aid. Mayor Lindsay appointed a committee of six, headed by McGeorge Bundy (president of the Ford Foundation), to prepare the plan. The committee's report, generally referred to as the "Bundy Report," was submitted to the Mayor in November, 1967.[43] It recommended that the present system be divided into thirty to sixty almost autonomous districts, each governed by a local community board. Each local board would be comprised of eleven members, five appointed by the mayor from a list provided by the central school authority and six elected by the parents of the district. Each local board would have the power to

---

[42] The teachers particularly objected to Herman Ferguson, who was at the time under indictment for plotting to murder Roy Wilkins, Whitney Young, Jr. and others. The other appointed principals had impeccable backgrounds.

[43] The formal title is *Reconnection for Learning: A Community School System for New York City* (New York: The Mayor's Advisory Panel on Decentralization, 1967).

select and dismiss personnel, establish curricula, and execute its own budget. Funds for the budget would be allocated to the board on the basis of need by a new, but limited, central authority. This central authority would be responsible for carrying out collective bargaining with the teachers' union and supervisory associations, long-range planning, conducting cost-effectiveness studies, and operating special schools. Other recommendations stressed development of local innovations and dismantling of the present bureaucracy.

These proposals were strongly attacked by the teachers' union and the Board of Education. Albert Shanker, president of the U.F.T., declared that adoption of the Bundy Report would result in "years of chaos and eventual destruction of the city's school system." He referred to the personnel provision in the plan as "the greatest piece of political patronage ever perpetuated."[44] In its critique of the report, the U.F.T. assailed all of the major provisions, essentially on the grounds that the proposals would undermine academic freedom and professional integrity by placing too much authority in the hands of community laymen. The union also maintained that "under the Bundy Plan, collective bargaining would become a chaotic mess," since the U.F.T. would be limited to collective bargaining on a city-wide basis while many vital decisions would be made at the community level. Perhaps fundamentally, teacher opposition boiled down to the fact that, from their perspective, "the Bundy report ignores the new power and integrity of the professional teacher who will not continue to teach in any school or district where professional decisions are made by laymen."[45]

The adoption of a negative attitude toward the Bundy plan, in conjunction with earlier events and with a vigorous lobbying campaign launched by the union to defeat state legislation on decentralization, convinced community control proponents that the teachers' union was determined to thwart any meaningful changes. These developments, combined with numerous difficulties the Ocean Hill board and its supervisor, Rhody McCoy, experienced in dealing with the Board of Education and the bureaucracy, contributed to an ever-increasing level of frustration in the Ocean Hill district.

Events came to a head on May 9, 1968, when the Ocean Hill-Brownsville Governing Board informed ten teachers and nine administrators that their employment in the district was terminated and that they were to report to central headquarters for reassignment. Much confusion

---

44 *New York Times*, November 10, 1967. In the same article the Board of Education also stated that the personnel provisions in the Bundy Report would result in "personal and politically motivated appointments on a large scale."

45 *U.F.T. Looks at School Decentralization, op. cit.*, p. 6.

centers around whether it was possible to arrange quietly voluntary transfers for the nineteen persons involved, and the exact charges underlying their transfers. But the specifics soon became overwhelmed as the incident touched off a major conflict over the amount of authority vested in the local board. When Superintendent Donovan ordered the nineteen educators back to the district, they were blocked from entering the schools and policemen had to escort them into the buildings. Parents, in turn, boycotted the schools for two days and community residents and teachers clashed outside school buildings. The U.F.T. declared a strike within the district and 350 of the approximately 500 teachers in the district walked out in support of the ten transferred teachers. Union news releases stated that the teachers had been "fired" (not transferred) without due process and demanded that written charges be filed, although it was not necessary under the existing rules to do so for any sort of transfer, voluntary or involuntary. After pressure was applied by the Board of Education and the union, the local board finally did file written charges against the teachers, but refused to reinstate them until their cases were officially determined. Thereupon, the U.F.T. called a district-wide strike for the last six weeks of the school year.

During the summer the charges were brought before Judge Francis E. Rivers, one of the city's few Negro judges, for a ruling. On August 26, Judge Rivers handed down his decision, which denied Supervisor McCoy and the local board the right to transfer out any of the ten teachers involved. The Ocean Hill governing board, however, voted not to accept the findings and maintained its position that the ten teachers could not teach in the district (the nine administrators had by this time transferred). The governing board had also proceeded to recruit new teachers, 75 per cent of whom were white and most of whom were Jewish, to replace the 350 teachers who had struck the district in May. The U.F.T., the Board of Education and Superintendent Donovan all, of course, insisted that the ruling by Rivers be implemented.

When school opened on September 9, the U.F.T. called the first of three city-wide strikes to enforce the reinstatement of the ten teachers. An almost predictable pattern developed in which an agreement between the contestants was supposedly reached, the teachers returned to work, were harassed and intimidated in the schools, and then the union declared the agreement violated and called another strike. Accompanying the U.F.T. strikes and community counter-protests were intensified black and Puerto Rican antagonisms toward the police for escorting the teachers, anti-Semitic epithets directed against

Jewish teachers and supervisory personnel, racial slurs hurled against Ocean Hill residents, and the virtual breakdown of governance in the New York City school system.[46] Between September and November, 1968, the New York schools were closed for 36 out of 48 days, except in the Ocean Hill district where the schools continued to operate during the strikes, and the city's atmosphere became electrified with hostility in all quarters.

The settlement which was finally reached called for the New York State Board of Education to establish a State Trustee to oversee the operation of Ocean Hill-Brownsville, and to assure the return of the union teachers to their classrooms. A three-man State Supervisory Commission was created which would protect the rights of teachers in all New York schools and would be empowered to close any school where teachers' rights were violated. Most observers considered the settlement a victory for the teachers' union, but one that came at an extremely high price for all involved.

Throughout the conflict, the union insisted that teachers' rights and due process were at the core of the controversy, while community backers maintained that the union was using the due process issue as a smokescreen for subverting any movement toward community control. Regardless of the interpretation, the New York struggle over community control has important implications for the governance of education in New York and other cities. Indeed, it has been suggested that the Ocean Hill controversy is "merely the opening round in what is destined to become a long and protracted struggle for control of public education."[47] School board members and administrators will obviously be involved in such a struggle, but the New York situation suggests that the major combat may occur between teacher organizations and community groups. Supporting this prediction is the notion that, at the very time teacher organizations across the nation have finally begun to wrestle some power away from the central administration and school board, and to enhance their status as professionals, community groups have appeared on the scene to demand a significant role in policy-making, which teachers feel is a threat to their recently hard-won

---

46 The New York school system has a large proportion of Jewish administrators and teachers. Consequently, as the conflict between the Ocean Hill community, largely composed of blacks and Puerto Ricans, and the educational establishment intensified, extremists in both camps introduced highly emotional racial and religious issues. However, it is important to note that many of the teachers who continued to work in the Ocean Hill district throughout the three strikes were white, Jewish teachers.

47 Arthur E. Salz, "Local Control vs. Professionalism," *Phi Delta Kappan* (February, 1969), pp. 332-334.

victories. The growth of teacher professionalism and the push for self-determination on the part of minority groups are two forces which are on a collision course that will inevitably result in extensive conflict and may reduce further the quality of education provided for minority group students. Such a development would be particularly unfortunate according to those who feel that a coalition between teacher organizations and community groups is an essential factor in reforming public education so that it does meet the needs of minority students.[48]

There is some evidence to suggest that such a coalition can be forged. The Washington Teachers Union, for example, has recently issued a report based on its two-year experience with an experimental district. In part, the report states:

> We envision that the opportunity for creative teaching approaches can be best implemented in those schools which are free from the control of the downtown administration. . . Certainly the central administration can be of assistance, but it will be based on terms laid down by the community and the teachers.

Commenting on the issues of job security, due process for teachers, and contract negotiations, the report states that the union is willing to work with the community

> . . . in establishing criteria for personnel selection and evaluation. Furthermore, the union will gladly sit down at the bargaining table to negotiate sub-contracts with local school boards. We believe that this kind of local bargaining affords both the community and the union the opportunity to engage in a creative and exciting bargaining experience that has not been tried by a single teacher organization in the country. Finally, the WTU Executive Board believes that the uniting of teacher power and community power shall create such a significant force in the district that we can begin to accomplish essential changes that will benefit [all students].[49]

To some extent, then, the future of community control may depend upon whether teacher organizations in other cities move in the direction adopted by the WTU or the position taken by the U.F.T. Teacher unions and community residents will no doubt clash from time to time under either model; however, the possibilities for establishing some

---

[48] See Brooks, *op. cit.*, pp. 39-40.
[49] Quoted in Nat Hentoff, "Ocean Hill-Brownsville and the Future of Community Control," *Civil Liberties* (February, 1969), pp. 4-5.

sort of "acceptable" balance would appear greater in a situation where the union accepts significant community participation as legitimate and is seeking a coalition against the "downtown establishment." Although it is not possible at this time to forecast how the issue of community control will be resolved in the cities, it is clear from the activities in New York, Washington, and elsewhere, that both teacher organizations and community organizations are on the educational scene to stay and will be major participants in educational policy-making.[50] The key question, of course, is whether these two groups will work in harmony to reform the public school system or whether teacher organizations will ally themselves with the establishment to protect the *status quo.*

V. Summary

This chapter focuses on three trends which have played, and will continue to play, an important role in widening the participation of previously powerless groups in city school politics. In recent years, teacher groups, after many decades of docile subordination, have made a vigorous effort to gain an equal voice in school matters. In seeking this goal, the teachers have altered the prevailing power configuration in numerous city school systems. Boards of education and administrators have found it increasingly difficult to operate the educational system in the closed fashion that existed for many years.

Complementing the assault leveled against the "educational establishment" by teachers has been the attempt by civil rights organizations, parent groups, and community groups to carve out a share of power. Although they generally failed to achieve their objectives in the struggle for integrated schools, their participation has undermined the position of professional educators and stimulated the shift toward making community control the battlecry. Indeed, the push for community control has become so potent that some teacher organizations consider it a threat to their newly-acquired status.

These developments have had some effect on changing the nature of school policy-making, particularly on whose interests are voiced and on the possibilities of introducing change, but no substantial change in policy outcome is yet definite. The low quality of education provided for minority group students still remains the most glaring and

---

[50] For a brief description of the quest for local control of schools in other cities, see Tim Parsons, "Community Control Across the Nation," *Community* (February, 1969), pp. 1-2.

pressing problem of city schools. Somewhat wider participation and slight innovation at the local level will not be enough to resolve this problem. Among other things, the possibilities of improvement are restricted not only by local conditions but also by the fiscal resources supplied intergovernmentally and by the amount of educational innovation stimulated by the state and federal levels of government. In the following two chapters we will discuss the roles of the state and federal government in their relation to the problems of urban education.

State Government and Schools

5

I. Introduction

Responsibility for the shortcomings of public education in our core cities does not rest solely with local schoolmen. Although much authority has been delegated to them, the ultimate power and authority over local school districts rest with the state government, for, constitutionally, the basic responsibility for providing public education is a state function, not a local or federal function.[1] Only the state, for example, has the authority to grant local communities permission to establish school districts or alter their boundaries. The state is also substantially involved in financing local schools, setting local school tax and debt limits, standardizing educational quality, establishing criteria for teacher training, certification, welfare measures, reorganization of districts, and racial integration of local schools.

---

[1] Since the Constitution contains no explicit statement about education, Constitutional authorities believe that educaion is a state function. This belief is based on Article Ten of the Constitution, which states: "The powers not delegated to the United States by the Constitution, nor prohibited by it to the States, are reserved to the States respectively, or to the people." All but six of the 50 state constitutions contain provisions for public education. For a review of court cases on this subject, see Arthur E. Wise, *Rich Schools, Poor Schools: The Promise of Equal Educational Opportunity* (Chicago: University of Chicago Press, 1968), pp. 93-120.

How have the states utilized this authority? To what extent has state action intensified or alleviated urban educational problems? What are the prospects for educational innovation at the state level? These are the questions we will deal with in this chapter. First we will discuss the structure of state educational decision-making and the key actors. Second, we will include the basic criticisms which have been leveled at the system. Then we will examine one of the key dimensions of state involvement: the provision and allocation of state aid for education. Finally, we will speculate on future state action in response to the problems of city schools.

II. State Education Structure and Actors

The existence of 50 separate states results in a wide variety of patterns of state education structure. There is enough similarity among the states, however, to make a general description possible.

As with all state functions, the state legislature retains the final authority to collect revenue and allocate expenditures among the range of public services. In fact, decisions regarding the level of financial support for schools generally constitute the primary involvement of state legislatures (and governors) in educational policy-making. Obviously, state legislatures are also involved in nonfiscal educational decisions, but for the most part they have delegated substantial discretionary power to other state bodies and generally follow the recommendations of these bodies when they make educational policy.[2] To explain this pattern, researchers often point out that most state legislators work only part-time, are poorly paid, lack competent staffs, and fail to develop expertise in policy areas. Historically, school matters have provided little political mileage for ambitious legislators.[3] As a result, the major influence over state education policy has fallen to state boards of education, state superintendents of education, and state departments of education.

---

[2] Robert H. Salisbury, "State Politics and Education" in Herbert Jacob and Kenneth N. Vines (ed.), *Politics in American States* (Boston: Little, Brown and Co., 1965), p. 339.

[3] On the shortcomings of state legislatures see Roscoe C. Martin, *The Cities and the Federal System* (New York: Atherton Press, 1966), Chapter Three; Terry Sanford, *Storm Over the States* (New York: McGraw-Hill, 1967); and Malcolm E. Jewell and Samuel C. Patterson, *The Legislative Process in the United States* (New York: Random House, 1966). On the lack of political mileage in education see Nicholas H. Masters, Robert H. Salisbury, Thomas H. Eliot, *State Politics and the Public Schools* (New York: Alfred A. Knopf, 1964), pp. 275-276.

State boards of education exist in all but three states (Michigan, Illinois, and Wisconsin). While their duties and influence vary from state to state, the boards are charged with the general supervision of elementary and secondary education. In 24 states, they are responsible for selecting the state superintendent. They usually present recommendations on school matters to the governor and legislature, formulate a proposed education budget for the governor, and appoint the professional staff of the state education department, usually upon the recommendation of the state superintendent. Most boards are composed of laymen, rather than professional educators, appointed by the governor, although in ten states, board members are popularly elected. In some states the boards are highly influential in determining educational policy. The New York Board of Regents, for example, "enjoys independent executive, legislative, and judicial power of such scope as to bring into question its consonance with American constitutional principles of separation of powers and checks and balances."[4] The more common pattern, however, is one in which the boards do not exercise much independent influence. In their study of eight northeastern states, Bailey and his colleagues concluded that boards "are less independent forces in their own right than sympathetic responders to the executive and administrative officials they oversee. . . . The rule is that strong commissioners of education, exercising forceful professional leadership, have a ready sounding-board and supporting officialdom in their state boards."[5] Thus, as with state legislatures, state boards are generally less influential in determining the specifics of educational policy than their formal authority might suggest.

Closer to the center of power is the chief state school officer (generally called superintendent or commissioner) and the state department of education which he heads. The authority of the superintendent varies, from state to state, but in general he and his department perform two broad functions. First, they provide a wide variety of technical services, advice and information to local school officials. Second, they establish and enforce minimum standards for local schools in such areas as curriculum, school calendar, teacher certification, school construction, pupil admissions and promotions, and graduation requirements.[6] Unlike state board members, state superintendents and state

---

[4] Stephen K. Bailey, Richard T. Frost, Paul E. Marsh, Robert C. Wood, *Schoolmen and Politics* (Syracuse: Syracuse University Press, 1962), p. 27.

[5] *Ibid.*, p. 27. Also see James D. Koerner, *Who Controls American Education?* (Boston: Beacon Press, 1968), pp. 83-91.

[6] Salisbury, *op. cit.*, pp. 337-338.

education department personnel are invariably professional educators themselves with strong ties to the profession. The combination of professional credentials and the fact that state education departments administer the distribution of state aid provides the superintendent and his agency with two important levers in influencing state education practices. Local districts must meet the set standards in order to qualify for much-needed aid. Consequently, state education administrators have traditionally dominated local districts in terms of personnel standards, and have been extremely influential in shaping university training programs for prospective teachers. On the issue of teacher training, critics accuse state schoolmen of stressing trivial courses in pedagogy rather than a program of substantial intellectual substance as the significant component of teacher training.[7] Teacher training programs have been strongly criticized for preparing virtually all teachers to teach in white, middle-class schools and for ignoring the preparation of teachers for ghetto schools. Only recently have colleges of education begun to develop programs to train teachers especially for ghetto schools and to make a conscious effort to recruit black college students.

The criticisms leveled at teacher training are only part, though an important part, of a more sweeping attack that has been lodged against state schoolmen.[8] In general, they are accused of being an important component (and in some sense a "tool") of an "interlocking directorate" of professional educational groups and interests, often referred to as the "educationalists." The critics argue that the educationalists monopolize the colleges of education and thus the training of teachers and administrators. This control determines who shall teach, what shall be taught, what is "acceptable" educational policy, and the probability of innovation. An important premise in this argument is that all the key educationalists are protectors of the *status quo* and are active in the state affiliates of the NEA, which generally operates as the most important school interest group in the state and wields a great deal of influence in preventing change.

Although this notion may be overstated, particularly in view of the great variety among the states, evidence suggests that such a situation

---

[7] James B. Conant, *The Education of American Teachers* (New York: McGraw-Hill, 1963), and James D. Koerner, *The Miseducation of American Teachers* (Boston: Houghton Mifflin Co., 1963).

[8] See for example: Arthur E. Bestor, *Educational Wastelands* (Urbana: University of Illinois Press, 1953); Arthur E. Bestor, *The Restoration of Learning* (New York: Alfred A. Knopf, 1955); Hyman Rickover, *Education and Freedom* (New York: E. P. Dutton, 1959); James B. Conant, *Shaping Educational Policy* (New York: McGraw-Hill, 1964); and James D. Koerner, *Who Controls American Education, op. cit.*

does exist in some states. Masters and his colleagues reached the conclusion that:

> . . . in each of the states we surveyed the major group was the state affiliate of the National Education Association; namely, the MSTA in Missouri, the IEA in Illinois, and the MEA in Michigan. These groups have a relatively high degree of organization, a principal spokesman, a wealth of information about school needs, and generally favorable access to at least some point in the *formal* decision-making structure. . . . In each state surveyed, legislators frequently singled out the education interests as the most powerful in the state.[9]

Conant also comments on the influence of the state NEA and its relationship to the state education departments in his study of sixteen states. He writes:

> The major weakness of all the state departments of education I have encountered, with perhaps one or two exceptions, is that they are too much a part of the educational establishment. That is, I found many of these agencies, unlike the regulatory commission at the Federal level, to be little more than the "willing tools" of the interests and clientele, particularly the education association (that is, the NEA state affiliate). In more than one state I heard highly placed education and political officials claim that state departments of education "follow a party line" or "reflect the public school mentality." These terms were used in a derogatory sense. A grave shortcoming of our educational leadership at the state level, in my opinion, is often its unwillingness or incapacity to respond to forces outside the establishment.[10]

The prevalence of such circumstances at the state level carries important implications for city school systems. In many states, leaders in both the state education department and the state NEA have been recruited primarily from rural school districts and are, therefore, rurally oriented. Gittell and Hollander concluded that "state education departments have been ill-equipped to deal with the problems of large urban cities. Their organization and programs have been concerned primarily with the problems of rural and suburban districts. Only recently have any of the large states even considered a new role for themselves in relation to large city districts. None of the departments have city divisions or specialists in urban problems."[11] The rural backgrounds of many state schoolmen, combined with the fact that city

---

[9] Masters, *op. cit.*, pp. 268-271.
[10] *Shaping Educational Policy, op. cit.*, p. 37.
[11] *Six Urban School Districts* (New York: Frederick A. Praeger, Publishers, 1968), p. 121.

school systems are separated from the political system of the city and thus from city representatives in the legislature, puts city schoolmen at a disadvantage when they atempt to have their needs met at the state level. Since the leading state schoolmen have few ties with city districts, "the big city schools get a less sympathetic hearing in many states than do the outstate schools."[12] Again, this pattern varies considerably from state to state, but is supported by examining the distribution of state aid for local schools.

III. State School Aid

The first point to make concerning state education aid is that it constitutes the largest proportion of all state intergovernmental aid. As Table 9 illustrates, at the turn of the century, almost nine out of every ten dollars state governments distributed to local governments were expended for education. This relationship dipped by 1940, so that half of all state-aid dollars were spent for education. However, in the post-World War II period, education's share of state aid steadily increased, and by 1967 constituted two out of every three state-aid dollars. Much of this increase in the postwar period can be attributed to the baby boom and the subsequent "skyrocketing" of state aid for school con-

TABLE 9

State Education Aid As a Percent of All State
Intergovernmental Expenditures, 1902-1967

Year	Percent
1902	86.5
1922	64.7
1932	49.7
1940	42.3
1950	48.7
1960	57.8
1967	62.2

Source: U.S. Bureau of the Census, Census of Governments, 1967, Vol. 6. No. 4, *State Payments to Local Governments.*

---

[12] Salisbury, *op. cit.*, p. 345. Conant also found "a great reluctance on the part of some state education departments to concern themselves with the special problems of school districts in highly urbanized areas." *Shaping Educational Policy, op. cit.*, p. 38.

struction.[13] Local school districts, confronted simultaneously with relentless population growth and tax and debt limitations, were often rescued from fiscal disaster by state legislative grants for school building programs.

Despite the considerable proportion of state aid historically allocated to education, it was not until the depression decade and the postwar era that a fundamental shift occurred in financial support of local education. As Table 10 indicates, prior to the 1930's state aid amounted

TABLE 10

Percent of Revenue Received From Federal, State, and Local Sources For Public Elementary and Secondary Schools, 1920-1968

Year	Federal Sources	State Sources	Local Sources
1920	0.3	16.5	83.2
1930	0.4	16.9	82.7
1940	1.8	30.3	67.9
1950	2.8	39.8	57.4
1960	4.4	39.1	56.5
1968	7.7	40.3	52.0

Source: U.S. Bureau of the Census, *Historical Statistics of the United States and National Education Association, Financial Status of the Public Schools* (Washington, D.C. NEA, 1968).

to only 17 per cent of the revenue available to schools, and local revenue sources, basically the property tax, accounted for over 80 per cent of the money. During the depression, however, the contribution of state aid almost doubled, so that by 1940, about 30 per cent of school revenue was derived from the state. By 1968, the state's support share had increased to 40 per cent and the local share had decreased to approximately 50 per cent.

This shift toward larger state support reflects the institutionalization of so-called "foundation programs." The idea that each state should establish a foundation program was first developed and proselytized by a small group of faculty members at Teachers College, Columbia University. Basic to the foundation concept is the notion that all school districts throughout a state should expend a certain number of dollars per student to insure a minimum educational program. Since each local

---

[13] Bailey, *et al.*, pp. 17-18.

district differs in its ability to achieve minimum standards, state aid, under the foundation concept, is distributed according to an equalization principle—poorer districts receive relatively more than wealthy districts. State money is allocated by means of a formula, which generally includes consideration of: (1) the total number of dollars needed per student to support minimum standards; (2) a minimum financial effort on the part of local districts; (3) the tax resources of local districts; and (4) a state-wide equalization of property assessments so that local tax effort may be determined.[14]

Once again, it is important to note that there is much variation among the states. Some state programs are wholly equalizing, other states provide only flat grants to local districts, and the majority of states utilize a mixture of equalizing and flat grants. In general, however, the largest proportion of state aid is dispersed according to some equalizing measure.[15]

Not only do states differ in the way they distribute school aid, but the amount of money allocated to the average local district varies greatly from state to state. In 1962, for example, New York State supplied an average of $365 per pupil to local districts, Illinois allocated $112 per pupil, and Iowa provided only $55 per pupil.[16] Given this striking variation, it is somewhat surprising that few scholars have attempted to identify the reasons for the differences. Most of the studies dealing with the determinants of governmental expenditures have focused on the combination of state and local expenditures or just local expenditures; few studies have analyzed state expenditures separately. The most common finding when state-local school spending is used as the dependent variable is that wealth (median family income) and property valuation are the most powerful explanatory variables.[17] Although other factors account for a small portion of the

---

14 *Ibid.*, pp. 18-20.

15 Charles C. Benson, "State Aid Patterns" in Jesse Burkhead, *Public School Finance: Economics and Politics* (Syracuse: Syracuse University Press, 1964), pp. 208-209.

16 U.S. Bureau of the Census, *Census of Government, 1962, Vol. IV, No. 1, Finances of School Districts.*

17 Solomon Fabricant, *The Trend of Government Activity in the United States Since 1900* (New York: National Bureau of Economic Research, 1952); Glenn W. Fisher, "Determinants of State and Local Government Expenditures: A Preliminary Analysis," *National Tax Journal*, XIV (1961), 349-355; Richard E. Dawson and James A. Robinson, "Interparty Competition, Economic Variables, and Welfare Politics in the American States," *Journal of Politics* (May 1963), pp. 265-289; Seymour Sacks and Robert Harris, "The Determinants of State and Local Government Expenditures and Intergovernmental Flow of Funds," *National Tax Journal* (March 1964), pp. 75-85; and Thomas Dye, *Politics, Economics and the Public: Policy Outcomes in the American States* (Chicago: Rand McNally and Company, 1966).

variation, a recent study concludes that almost "70 per cent of the total variation among the fifty states in per pupil expenditures can be explained with reference to median family income."[18]

The only study which attempted to explain state education expenditures separately arrived at an opposite conclusion. It found that the relationships between economic characteristics and state spending tended to be negative.[19] The two most important determinants identified in the Sharkansky study were (1) the previous level of state spending and (2) the percentage of state and local expenditures made by the state government. This conclusion tends to beg the question, however, because it fails to determine what factors influence previous state spending and the state proportion of all state-local expenditures. In the latter relationship, evidence indicates that, generally, the state's share of all public school revenue is higher in the poorer and more rural states.[20] Apparently, the relatively lower amount of resources available locally in such states encourages greater state involvement in support of public services.

While most of the above studies rely heavily on socio-economic and governmental arrangement factors, political variables also play an important, if less obvious, role in shaping the nature of state aid for schools.[21] In their analysis of the politics of state aid, Bailey and his colleagues described the significance of the political context in the following manner:

> Strong executive and legislative leadership, active and well-staffed departments of education, disciplined political parties, elastic and broad-based state revenue laws, vigorous and coordinated educational pressure groups and the existence of rapid-growth factors in metropolitan areas appear to create a context favorable to the success of schoolmen. Conversely, where traditions of localism are strong, where political parties are lopsided and internally fragmented, where educational interest groups are divided, where populations are heavily rural and relatively stable, where tax-minded businessmen with the help of a conservative press create a strong ethos against state spending and state action, where executive and legislative leadership is weak and uncommitted, where state boards and state departments of education

---

[18] Dye, *ibid.*, p. 81.

[19] Ira Sharkansky, *Spending in the American States* (Chicago: Rand McNally and Company, 1968), pp. 60-73.

[20] Salisbury, *op. cit.*, p. 357.

[21] All of the above cited works found that such factors as party competition, voter participation, partisanship and malapportionment had little independent affect on expenditures when income is controlled. However, the significant variables do not explain the total variation. Consequently, it is possible that more subtle political variables are important in accounting for the residue variation.

are inadequately staffed and divided, where state revenue systems are rigid and unviable, schoolmen find rough sledding.[22]

According to this statement, an important aspect of the political context which improves the ability of schoolmen to achieve their objective is group cohesion. Salisbury also stresses this point. He notes that "schoolmen believe that in unity there is strength, and that the public schools will receive more state aid when schoolmen are unified."[23] In addition to this quest for unity is the emphasis that education issues be treated "non-politically," without conflict. Conventional political wisdom suggests that state schoolmen will be treated more favorably if they present their needs in a consensual and matter-of-fact manner. Such an approach tends to disarm state aid "depressants" and makes it more difficult for them to oppose school needs.[24] Some evidence suggests, however, that the search for unity and nonconflict may itself act as a depressant on school aid. In the Masters, *et. al.*, study, for example, it was found that Michigan, where schoolmen are divided and conflict is high, spends a higher share of its income per capita on schools than do Illinois or Missouri, where cohesion and nonconflict prevail. Apparently, one of the prices paid to achieve nonconflict is a tendency, as in Illinois and Missouri, to keep requests for school aid down to "acceptable" levels. In short, the factors affecting the level of state aid require further investigation. Not only are there questions surrounding the influence of socio-economic and political factors, but little attention has been paid to how new trends, such as teacher militancy, affect the level of state support.

IV. The Impact of State Aid

Determining what influences the amount of state school aid is an interesting inquiry, but a more important question concerns the impact of state aid on local schools. We have already noted, for instance, that state aid has been utilized as an effective lever for establishing and maintaining minimum standards in most states. In enforcing minimum standards, states have also used state aid to encourage local school consolidation. By dangling promises of state aid, the states were able to reduce the number of school districts from 127,000 in 1932 to about

---

22 *Schoolmen in Politics, op. cit.*, p. 104.
23 "State Politics and Education," *op. cit.*, p. 349.
24 Bailey, *et al.*, define "depressants" as groups or individuals who seek to keep state school aid from increasing. Contrary to a popular notion, they concluded that the Catholic Church, at least in the Northeast, was not a depressant.

32,000 in 1964. Those states that paid the largest proportion of the public school bill were also the states that were most successful in consolidating local districts.[25]

The case of school consolidation clearly illustrates that state aid can have an important impact on the nature of local schools, particularly when state schoolmen use aid as a means for carrying out a specific educational policy. Given this fact, it is instructive to analyze the impact of state aid on local fiscal support for schools. More specifically, to what extent do states utilize state aid to equalize educational opportunities in central cities as compared to suburbia?

In Chapter 2, we noted that in 1964, despite the relatively greater needs of city students, the 37 largest cities were spending, on the average, $124 less per pupil than their respective suburbs. This disparity results from two factors: first, family income, which is the most important determinant of local school expenditures, is lower in cities than it is in suburbs. In general, suburbs simply have greater levels of family wealth than cities. Second, state school aid is not allocated to overcome this difference. Instead, it actually flows in greater amounts to suburban schools (see Table 6). This enhances the ability of suburban districts to spend more per pupil than cities and contributes to the growing gap between suburban and city school expenditures. The relative disadvantage of city districts because of this pattern is compounded by the fact that they are in the same labor market as their surrounding suburbs.[26] Consequently, they are forced into competition with districts that have greater fiscal resources and, in many instances, better working conditions from the perspective of young, middle-class teacher graduates.

Suburban school districts generally receive more aid than city districts because most aid formulas rely upon property valuation per capita as the measure to establish the amount of community resources available to support education.[27] Several students of school finance argue, however, that per capita property valuation overstates the ability of cities to support schools.[28] Since cities must support a wider variety of noneducational public services than suburbs, the demands

---

[25] Dye, *op. cit.*, pp. 87-88.

[26] David C. Ranney, "The Determinants of Fiscal Support for Large City Educational Systems," *Administrators Notebook* (December, 1966), No. 4.

[27] Benson, *op. cit.*, p. 230.

[28] *Ibid.*; Ranney, *op. cit.*; Alan K. Campbell and Seymour Sacks, *Metropolitan America: Fiscal Patterns and Governmental Systems* (New York: Free Press, 1967); and Advisory Commission on Intergovernmental Relations, *Fiscal Balance in the American Federal System* (Washington, D.C.: U.S. Government Printing Office, 1967).

on the city tax base (which in many cases is stagnant or declining) are usually greater than in suburban communities. In addition to this "municipal overburden," it can be argued that there are several cost-increasing factors in city schools. City schools contain much larger proportions of students from low-income families who require special and costly educational programs. City schools also expend larger payments per teacher than suburban districts, because city districts generally have a larger proportion of older teachers who are at or near the maximum salary level. Finally, the site costs for schools are usually more expensive in cities than they are in suburbia, where land is more plentiful.

The combination of all these factors suggests that if state aid is viewed as a means for equalizing educational opportunity, then the formulas used for distributing aid within metropolitan areas must be reconsidered. Attention should focus on the appropriateness of using property valuation per capita as the sole community resource (median family income might also be considered), and on including some sort of "need" factor in formulas. For example, the federal 1965 Elementary and Secondary Education Act allocates funds to school districts on the basis of the proportion of students in families with incomes below $2,000.[29] As a result of this approach, the bulk of federal aid is distributed to city and poor rural districts, thus equalizing their capacity in relation to suburban districts.

Some scholars argue that the current allocation of state school aid and the resulting pattern of school expenditures is unconstitutional. They maintain that the disparities violate the equal-protection clause of the Fourteenth Amendment, and that the courts should order states to remedy the situation. Several court suits have been filed along these lines, but in April, 1969, the Supreme Court ruled that the Illinois state legislature could not be forced to equalize state school aid.[30]

The likelihood of states' redesigning their formulas along the lines established by the federal government does not appear promising, unless the Supreme Court reverses its 1969 ruling. The essentially rural orientation of the "educational establishment," particularly state education departments, in conjunction with the traditional rural domination

---

[29] The details of this act and the federal role in education are fully discussed in the following chapter. The Advisory Commission on Intergovernmental Relations has recommended that states include such a feature in their aid formulas. It has also recommended the establishment of county or regional school property taxing districts. See *Ibid.*, pp. 12-13.

[30] Wise, *Rich Schools, Poor Schools, op. cit.*, and the University of Chicago Center for Policy Study, *The Quality of Inequality: Urban and Suburban Public Schools* (Chicago: University of Chicago Press, 1968). For a summary of the Supreme Court decision see: *Law in Action* (March, 1969), p. 9.

in many state legislatures, works against major innovative legislation for urban schools. This is especially true when the legislation would tend to favor city schools at the "expense" of other school districts. On this point, many commentators viewed state legislative reapportionment, resulting from the Supreme Court ruling of *Reynolds v. Sims*, as a major breakthrough which would make the states more responsive to city needs. Leaving aside the question of whether rural interests did dominate state legislatures in the past or whether urban representatives failed to act cohesively, the important point for future state action is that reapportionment is more likely, because of postwar population trends, to increase suburban representation in state legislatures than city representation.[31] Therefore, the possibilities of altering state aid formulas would hinge on whether suburban legislators allied themselves with rural or city legislators on such an issue. Thus far, there is little evidence that suburban representatives are favorable to city needs or that reapportionment in general has made state capitals any more sympathetic to city officials.[32]

In conclusion, then, it is clear that while state aid certainly provides essential support for city schools, it also tends to intensify the relative disadvantage of city schools, and therefore, the unequal educational opportunity provided for city students. The political realities of the situation suggest that this pattern is unlikely to be radically altered in the near future.

V. The State and Ghetto Students

State action on the issue of school desegregation also illustrates the propensity of state schoolmen to be nonresponsive to the special problems of core city school systems. A brief review of state reactions to the basic theory underlying the 1954 Supreme Court ruling on school segregation supports this conclusion.

In the case of *Brown v. Board of Education*, the court held that school segregation by the states was a denial of equal protection of the laws and thus forbidden by the Fourteenth Amendment. Regarding

---

[31] On the complexity of the urban-rural split see: David R. Derge, "Metropolitan and Outside Alignments in Illinois and Missouri Legislative Delegation," *American Political Science Review* (December, 1958), p. 1051, and Robert S. Friedman, "The Urban-Rural Conflict Revisited," *The Western Political Quarterly* (June, 1961), pp. 481-495. Also see Robert Friedman, "The Reapportionment Myth," *National Civic Review* (April, 1960), pp. 184-188.

[32] See, for example, Samuel K. Gove, *Reapportionment and the Cities: The Impact of Reapportionment on Urban Legislation in Illinois* (Chicago: Center for Research and Urban Government, Loyola University, 1968).

the impact of segregated schooling on Negro students, Chief Justice Warren wrote: "To separate them from others of similar age and qualifications solely because of their race generates a feeling of inferiority as to their status in the community that may affect their hearts and minds in a way unlikely ever to be undone. Separate educational facilities are inherently unequal." Although the court ruling was directed against the practice of *de jure* segregation in southern states, the concept that segregated education is inherently unequal because it breeds feelings of inferiority was applied by civil rights groups to the widespread condition of *de facto* segregation in the North. In both regions of the country, however, the states have done little to eradicate segregated education.

Southern states were ordered by the Supreme Court to desegregate with "all deliberate speed," yet, by 1967, the vast majority of black students were still attending segregated schools.[33] Some southern school districts chose to shut down their public schools rather than integrate, but most simply devised strategies such as "freedom of choice" plans to accomplish token integration and forestall federal action.

An assessment of northern state action is complicated by the legal status of *de facto* segregation. Whether the *Brown* decision that "separate educational facilities are inherently unequal" only outlawed compulsory segregation or also applied to all school segregation, regardless of its source, is unclear. Several conflicting decisions have been handed down by federal district and appellate courts, but as of 1969 the Supreme Court had not ruled on the legal status of *de facto* segregation.[34] Despite the legal ambiguities concerning the source of segregation, the fact of segregated education in the North is predominate, and there is no evidence that its impact on black students is any less damaging than southern style segregation. During the decade following the *Brown* decision, before school integration was being replaced by community control as the prevailing goal of the black community, few northern state officials displayed interest in the impact of *de facto* segregation on black students or took action to eradicate it. In most cases, state officials simply ignored the issue unless local conflicts forced state involvement.

---

[33] U.S. Commission on Civil Rights, *Southern School Desegregation* (Washington, D.C.: U.S. Government Printing Office, 1968).

[34] One of the most controversial decisions on this topic was issued by Federal District Judge J. Skelly Wright in *Hobsen v. Hansen.* Judge Wright ruled that the Washington, D.C. school officials had denied black students equal educational opportunities through a variety of segregating practices and ordered them to take affirmative action to desegregate.

In a few states, however, some initiative was taken at the state level. The Commissioner of Education in New York State issued a directive in 1963 to all school systems, requesting that they submit a report on the racial composition of their schools and a statement of plans to redress racial imbalance. Although racial imbalance has increased in virtually all New York State school systems since the Commissioner's action, the state has not leveled any sanctions against school districts or provided any special incentives for districts that do integrate. In 1965, the Illinois state legislature passed the Armstrong Act, which called for local school districts to revise existing school attendance boundaries so as to minimize racial imbalance. In 1967, however, the Illinois Supreme Court ruled the law unconstitutional on the grounds that race could not be used as a means for administering educational programs.[35] Thus far, Massachusetts has taken the strongest state action on the issue of desegregation.[36] The racial imbalance law enacted by the Massachusetts legislature in 1965 is the first of its kind in the United States. Under the law, a racially imbalanced school is one with a student composition of over 50 per cent nonwhites. If such a condition exists in local school districts and officials fail to take steps to remedy the situation, they run the risk of losing state education funds. The law also authorizes incentive funds to local school districts that take positive steps to alleviate imbalance. Implementation of the law, however, has not been an easy task. The Boston school district, for example, submitted three plans for reducing imbalance but all three were rejected by the State Education Department. In response, the Boston school district filed suit to test the constitutionality of the law. While the state awaits a decision, the schools have become even more racially segregated. Despite some positive steps in the Springfield school district, segregation continued to increase, resulting in the state's suspending $6 million in state aid funds. If the law is eventually implemented, Massachusetts will be the first and only state to condition state funds upon local desegregation efforts.

The general failure of state governments to deal with segregated education during the 1950's and 1960's means that, with further population shifts, it will be even more difficult, if not impossible, to eliminate segregated education in the 1970's. Consequently, any future

---

[35] "Affirmative Integration: Studies of Efforts to Overcome *De Facto* Segregation in the Public Schools," *Law and Society* (November, 1967), pp. 102-103.

[36] An interesting case study of the enactment of the Massachusetts law can be found in James Bolner and Robert A. Shanley, *Civil Rights in the Political Process: An Analysis of the Massachusetts Racial Imbalance Law of 1965* (Amherst: Bureau of Government Research, University of Massachusetts, 1967).

efforts by states to improve the quality of education for black students will undoubtedly occur within the framework of segregated educational systems. With segregation as a basic fact, the states would be faced with compensatory education and community control, or some combination of the two, as the primary means for improving ghetto education. Unfortunately, there is little evidence to suggest that state policymakers will be any more innovative along these lines than they have been in integration.

Evaluations of compensatory educational programs indicate that they have been generally unsuccessful.[37] One criticism leveled against most compensatory educational programs, in addition to their being segregated, is that the amount of resources available has been meager.[38] In most programs the per-pupil expenditures have not been much greater than the expenditures in normal programs. While additional funds are not the only factor in making compensatory education successful, the level of expenditures does make a difference, and state governments generally have not fortified compensatory programs in the past. At present, it appears unlikely that they will do so in the near future, for the same reasons that they are unlikely to modify their state aid formulas.

The only state thus far to establish a policy on the issue of community control is New York State. In response to the decentralization controversy discussed in Chapter 4, the New York State legislature enacted a law in April, 1969, which favored the opponents of community control. The legislation abolished the three demonstration districts and established 30 to 33 community school boards which would have the power to hire a district superintendent and fix his salary; to select textbooks from a centrally approved list; and to contract for repair and maintenance up to $250,000 a year. However, the central board (to consist of seven members, five elected from the boroughs and two appointed by the mayor) and administration will retain control over the general budget, all high schools, the licensing and assignment of personnel, and will have the power to institute many changes, including the elimination of local school boards. The only exception to the personnel provision would be in those schools where average reading scores fall below a certain level. In such a situation, the local board would be able to hire teachers not on the central list, provided they pass the central authority's test or the National Teachers

---

[37] U.S. Commission on Civil Rights, *Racial Isolation in the Public Schools* (Washington, D.C.: U.S. Government Printing Office, 1967).

[38] Albert Shanker, "What's Wrong With Compensatory Education?" *Saturday Review* (January 11, 1969), pp. 56-61.

Examination.[39] Although New York is usually regarded as a progressive state, the action of its legislature signals that the proponents of community control in New York and elsewhere are unlikely to receive much assistance at the state level.

Thus, in the areas of fiscal support, integration, compensatory education, and community control, the states have taken few steps to upgrade the quality of education provided for ghetto students. If the past is any clue to the future, one can only conclude that the odds are against significant changes at the state level in response to the pressing education problems of the cities.

VI. Summary

Constitutionally, state governments have the primary authority to perform the education function. Generally, the states have not been particularly sensitive to urban educational problems. To some extent, this lack of sensitivity can be traced to the *status quo* posture of state governments, but the pattern of educational decision-making at the state level and the orientation of decision-makers are also significant. In distribution of state aid, rather than working to equalize the widening gap between suburban school expenditures and city expenditures, the states increase the gap by allocating relatively larger amounts to the suburbs. Only a few states have attempted to eliminate segregated education within their boundaries, and those few states have been largely unsuccessful. States have provided little support for compensatory education programs and the only state to establish a policy on community control acted to retain the great bulk of power in the hands of the established bureaucracy. There is little evidence to suggest that the record of the states will be altered in the near future. Whether the same conclusion also applies to the federal government is the topic treated in the following chapter.

---

[39] *New York Times,* May 4, 1969, and Joseph Featherstone, "The Albany Stranglers: Choking off Community Schools," *The New Republic* (July 19, 1969), pp. 16-18. It is interesting to note that one of the few powers provided to local boards, letting contracts for $250,000, indicates that many sub-issues are involved in the general decentralization issue. This small provision was apparently included as a response to the fact that ghetto residents deeply resent that contracts are let to contractors and unions that discriminate against blacks and Puerto Ricans. The concession is small, however; it amounts to only 7 per cent of $110 million spent for maintenance and construction.

The Federal Government and Education 6

I. Introduction

Although state governments are primarily responsible for providing education, federal involvement in support of education goes back to the beginnings of the nation. Even before the United States Constitution was adopted in 1789, the federal government had already taken two important steps to promote public education. Under the Land Ordinance of 1785, Congress set aside a lot in each township of the Northwest Territory for maintaining public schools, and in the Northwest Ordinance of 1787, established a policy which stated: "Religion, morality, and knowledge, being necessary to good government and the happiness of mankind, schools and the means of education shall forever be encouraged."

During the following century, the federal government encouraged development of public education through the mechanism of land grants. As each state entered the union, two sections (sometimes four sections) of each township were set aside for schools. In 1862, Congress enacted the Morrill Act, which provided grants of federal land to each state for establishing colleges specializing in agriculture and mechanical arts. The original legislation authorized to the state 30,000 acres of land, or the equivalent in scrip for each congressman in the state. The law was first amended in 1890, and several times afterward, to include annual grants to "land grant colleges" for operating costs. As of 1964, there were 67 such colleges in operation throughout the nation.[1] Five years after the passage of the first Morrill Act, the federal concern for education was further illustrated by the establishment of a Department of Education.

Throughout the first-half of the twentieth century, the federal government's role in education was expanded considerably. In 1917, Congress enacted the Smith-Hughes Act, which "stands as one of the first examples of federal aid provided to schools below the college level."[2] The legislation provided federal grants-in-aid to promote improvement of vocational education. Federal funds were supplied to support courses and teacher training programs in the fields of agriculture, home economics, trades and industries. During the depression decade, Congress passed several laws encouraging educational activities as part of the general relief program. The Public Works Administration furnished loans and grants for school construction; the Civilian Conservation Corps provided vocational training for unemployed young men; and the Federal Emergency Relief Administration supplied funds for unemployed teachers and developed adult education programs. The Lanham Act was passed in 1941 to aid communities that had unusual population increases in military personnel and defense workers. Some funds were provided "in lieu of taxes" to compensate for military installations not on the local tax rolls, and other funds were furnished for school construction and operation. This law was the forerunner of the current "impacted areas" school aid program, which supplied $521 million to local schools in 1968.[3] The Service Man's Readjustment Act (commonly known as the GI Bill) was passed in 1944. It provided education and training for approximately eight million veterans of World War II. A modified extension of the law was also enacted to finance the education of veterans of the Korean and Vietnam Wars.

Despite this wide variety of support for education, the federal government did not establish a general aid program for elementary and secondary education until 1965, although numerous proposals had

---

[1] Congressional Quarterly Service, *Federal Role in Education* (Washington, D.C.: Congressional Quarterly, 1965), p. 16.

[2] Sidney W. Tiedt, *The Role of the Federal Government in Education* (New York: Oxford University Press, 1966), p. 23.

[3] Congressional Quarterly, Inc., *C. Q. Almanac* (Washington, D.C.: Congressional Quarterly, Inc., 1968), p. 594.

been set forth for almost a century.[4] The first such proposal was submitted by Representative George F. Hoar (R., Mass.) in 1870. Educational groups denounced the Hoar Bill as unwarranted federal interference in local schools, and it was eventually withdrawn. In virtually every congressional session after 1870, however, some sort of general aid program for elementary and secondary education was proposed. Prior to 1965, none of the proposals was enacted, because each became embroiled in some combination of such controversial issues as the need for federal assistance, the fear of federal control of education, the granting of federal funds to segregated schools, the distribution of federal aid to private educational institutions, and the allocation of federal funds among the states.[5]

This chapter focuses on the post-World War II obstacles which prevented passage of a general federal aid program before 1965; the factors contributing to passage of the 1965 Education Act; the impact of the 1965 Act and other "Great Society" legislation on urban schools; the continuing controversies surrounding federal aid to schools; and the possible future role of the federal government in helping to resolve the urban education crisis.

II. Obstacles to Federal School Aid, 1945–1965[6]

One strategy often utilized by proponents of a new governmental program is that of relating their proposed program to the alleviation

---

[4] The exact meaning of "general aid" is ambiguous. However, it generally has been used in the school-aid debate during the postwar years to refer to aid for school construction and for teacher salaries as opposed to aid for highly specialized educational activities, such as development of science courses or provision of school lunches.

[5] Discussions of the federal aid to education controversy prior to 1965 can be found in: Gordon Canfield Lee, *The Struggle for Federal Aid First Phase: A History of the Attempts to Obtain Federal Aid for Common Schools, 1870-1890* (New York: Columbia University Teachers College, 1949); Anne Gibson Buis, *An Historical Study of the Role of the Federal Government in the Financial Support of Education, With Special Reference to Legislative Proposals and Action* (Unpublished doctoral dissertation, Ohio State University, 1953); Frank J. Munger and Richard F. Fenno, Jr., *National Politics and Federal Aid to Education* (Syracuse: Syracuse University Press, 1962); H. Douglas Price, "Race, Religion, and the Rules Committee" in Alan F. Westin (ed.), *The Uses of Power* (New York: Harcourt, Brace and World, Inc., 1962); and Robert Bendiner, *Obstacle Course on Capitol Hill* (New York: McGraw-Hill, 1964).

[6] The following two sections are summarized from Philip Meranto, *The Politics of Federal Aid to Education in 1965. A Study in Political Innovation* (Syracuse: Syracuse University Press, 1967).

of some general societal "crisis." The supporters of federal aid to elementary and secondary education did not ignore the "crisis" strategy. Throughout the twentieth century, they attempted to utilize a variety of pressing social conditions to strengthen their quest for federal assistance. For example, they pointed to the high rate of selective service rejections because of illiteracy during both world war periods, in an attempt to dramatize the frequency of illiteracy in American society and the inadequacy of the response to this condition by the education system. During the post-World War II period, proponents of federal school aid stressed, above all else, teacher and classroom shortages and a series of interrelated conditions which they felt warranted broader federal support for education. Generally, their argument was presented in the following terms:

1. The education function is in a state of crisis resulting from the baby boom of the early 1940's and the postwar period in general. The impact of the baby boom is reflected in public school enrollment statistics which show that enrollment actually declined between 1930 and 1950, from 25.6 million to 25.1 million. By the school year 1959 to 1960, however, enrollment jumped to 36.1 million, an increase of about 43 per cent in one decade.[7]

2. The enrollment explosion has caused a serious shortage of classrooms; has increased the size of classes; and has contributed, along with low salaries, to the failure to attract and keep a sufficient number of qualified individuals in the profession of education.[8] Consequently, many schools are characterized by overcrowded conditions, operation of double shifts, and undermanned instructional staffs.

3. The federal government has a responsibility to help relieve these problems because of their implications for national welfare. National wealth and economic productivity have been related to the increased educational level of the population. A sound education system also underlies the nation's scientific and defense capabilities. The society has also become increasingly interdependent, particularly through the increased internal mobility of the work force and school population.

---

[7] Individuals testifying before Congressional committees have used a variety of statistics at different times to illustrate this trend. These figures are taken from: U.S. Department of Health, Education, and Welfare, Office of Education, *Digest of Educational Statistics* (Washington, D.C.: U.S. Government Printing Office, 1965), p. 10.

[8] Much debate centered around the statistics that are used to support these patterns. The National Education Association, for example, claimed that in 1961, there was a 140,000 classroom backlog. The U.S. Chamber of Commerce, on the other hand, argued that classroom construction was outstripping increased enrollment and that, if there was a shortage, it was much smaller. For both points of view see: U.S. House, Committee on Education and Labor, *Federal Aid to Schools*, 87th Cong., 1st Sess., 1961, pp. 165-70, 282-85.

Therefore, the quality of education in any one part of the country affects the rest of the society, and is therefore of national concern.

4. The federal government not only has a responsibility to provide general support for local schools, but it also has the necessary resources. Local communities and state governments have had their fiscal resources strained to the limit by demands for improved educational and noneducational services. With its superior tax base, the federal government is in a position to provide relief for state and local governments while simultaneously increasing the nation's potential through a strengthened educational system.[9]

Enrollment explosion, classroom shortage, teacher shortage, fiscal strain, and national well-being, then, constituted the basis of the proponent argument for general federal aid. The major interest groups which have consistently been proponents of the issue during the postwar period include: National Education Association*; AFL-CIO and its affiliates; American Federation of Teachers*; Council of Chief State School Officers*; National Council of Parent-Teachers; American Association of University Professors; American Association of University Women; Americans for Democratic Action; National Farmers' Union; American Parents Committee; American Veterans Committee; and the National Association for the Advancement of Colored People (only to nonsegregated schools). As indicated below, the cohesion of this proponent line-up varied considerably, depending upon the specific features of any bill, particularly as they related to aid for nonpublic schools and for segregated schools.

The groups opposed to federal school aid took strong exception to the reasoning of the proponents, and argued that the so-called "education crisis" was vastly overstated. First, they pointed out that while school enrollment between 1950-51 and 1960-61 increased by 44.4 per cent, the number of teachers increased by 51.9 per cent; that classroom teachers' salaries increased 70 per cent during the same period; and that between 1950 and 1960, new classrooms were built at the annual rate of 67,360, or 7,360 more than the needs projected by educational authorities.[10] Second, they maintained that public education is not a federal responsibility. The sphere of federal services and functions

---

[9] For a typical presentation of these arguments, see the testimony of Carl J. Megel, president of the American Federation of Teachers, before the House Committee on Education and Labor during 1961. *Ibid.*, p. 267.

* Although supporters of federal aid, these groups have opposed proposed legislation which included aid for nonpublic schools.

[10] These statistics were used by the National Association of Manufacturers before the Senate Committee in 1961. See U.S. Senate, Committee on Labor and Public Welfare, *Public School Assistance Act of 1961*, 87th Cong., 1st Sess., 1961, pp. 375-76.

should be limited to those matters that can be handled only by the federal government.[11] Third, they warned that federal aid would lead eventually to federal control of education:

> Federal subsidies mean federal decisions about school problems which should be left to states or their communities to make. . . While the present Congress may deny most sincerely any intention of federal "takeover" in education, subsequent Congresses will find that both more federal money and more federal direction are necessary.[12]

And finally, the traditional foes of aid asserted that, in contrast to the fiscal capacity of state governments, "the federal government is in a precarious financial situation." They pointed to the balance-of-payments problem, budget deficits, the public debt, and "crushing" federal tax rates as evidence, and asserted that the federal government should be retrenching, rather than extending, its financial commitments.

It is clear that neither set of arguments is more "valid" than the other, but rather, that they represent different perspectives on the same issue. Before 1965, however, the opponents of aid successfully defeated each attempt to pass school aid legislation. The opponent position was fortified by the split among proponents over the issues of religion, race, and the nature of aid; the characteristics of presidential leadership; and the structural features of Congress.

The Religious Issue

Whether federal school aid can and should be provided to nonpublic schools is a question which has historically plagued, and continues to plague, the whole relationship between the federal government and education. At the center of this controversy, particularly during the postward period, has been the National Catholic Welfare Conference, the organization which represents the Catholic Bishops. From 1919 to 1944, the N.C.W.C. officially opposed federal aid to education on the grounds that Catholic schools would suffer from the competition of a better-financed public school system and that aid would eventually

---

[11] *Ibid.* Proponents of federal aid maintain that Article I, Section 8 (the welfare clause), of the Constitution provides the basis for federal responsibility in the field of education.

[12] From the testimony of the U.S. Chamber of Commerce. See House Committee on Education and Labor, *Federal Aid to Schools*, pp. 282-285. Groups which have joined the Chamber of Commerce in opposition to federal aid include: Council of State Chambers of Commerce, National Association of Manufacturers, Southern State Industrial Council, National School Boards Association (opposed since 1961), Investment Bankers Association of America, American Farm Bureau, American Legion, and Daughters of the American Revolution.

necessitate the acceptance of federal control over Catholic schools. Presumably, the increased fiscal strain experienced by Catholics in their efforts to maintain a Catholic education system overshadowed these fears, because around 1945, the N.C.W.C. altered its view on the issue. Since that time, the N.C.W.C. has supported the concept of federal aid, but has strongly opposed any program that excluded assistance for nonpublic schools. The claim for aid is based on the argument that nonpublic schools perform the public function of educating about 7,000,000 students (in 1961) and of fulfilling the state requirements of compulsory education. Therefore, nonpublic schools deserve an equivalent share of any aid the federal government might provide for public schools. Further, private schoolmen maintain that such assistance would not violate the principle of separation of church and state since the Supreme Court has never explicitly ruled against the practice of the federal government's aiding individual private school children. The GI Bill of Rights is often cited as a precedent for providing aid to individual students who may attend the school of their choice.[13]

These arguments were vigorously challenged by the groups protesting the provision of federal funds to private and parochial schools. The opponents believed that such aid definitely violated the principle of separation of church and state as set forth in these opening words of the First Amendment to the Constitution: "Congress shall make no law respecting the establishment of religion or prohibiting the free exercise thereof." They maintain that federal support for nonpublic schools would be inconsistent with the no-establishment clause and, thus, unconstitutional. They refer to three court cases to buttress their position: *Everson v. Board of Education* in 1947, *McCollin v. Board of Education* in 1948, and *Zorach v. Clauson* in 1952. In all three instances, it was ruled that the government may not finance religious schools or religious education. Writing for the majority in the *Everson* case, Justice Hugo Black stated a view which has often been cited in this context: "No tax in any amount, large or small, can be levied to support any religious activities or institutions, whatever they may be called, or whatever form they may adopt to back or practice religion."[14]

The key groups that have sought federal aid but have opposed funds for nonpublic schools include education groups such as the National

---

[13] Neil G. McCluskey (S.J.), *Catholic Viewpoint on Education* (Garden City: Hanover House, 1959). The most reliable allies of the Catholic church on this issue have been labor organizations. See Munger and Fenno, *op. cit.*, pp. 61-62.

[14] Quoted in U.S. Senate, *Constitutionality of Federal Aid to Education in Its Various Aspects*, 87th Cong., 1st Sess., 1961, Document No. 29, p. 12.

Educational Association and the Council of Chief State School Officials, and religious organizations such as the American Jewish Congress, Baptist Joint Committee on Public Affairs, National Council of Churches, National Association of Evangelicals, National Lutheran Church, Protestants and Other Americans United for Separation of Church and State, and Unitarian Fellowship for Social Justice.

The House deliberations over federal aid to nonpublic schools became so heated in 1949 and 1950 that they stimulated a nationwide debate, which placed Mrs. Eleanor Roosevelt and Francis Cardinal Spellman on opposite sides of the issue. The controversy became so bitter both inside and outside Congress that the chances for passing a general aid bill became nil for several years. During the debate, a forecast of the fate awaiting federal aid under President Dwight Eisenhower was also revealed. As president of Columbia University, Eisenhower sent a letter to a subcommittee of the House Education and Labor Committee expressing approval of federal aid only to those areas where the tax-paying potential could not provide adequate education. He also remarked:

> I would flatly oppose any grant by the Federal government to all states in the union for educational purposes. . . . Unless we are careful even the great and necessary educational process in our country will become yet another vehicle by which the believer in paternalism, if not outright socialism, will gain still additional power for the central government.[15]

A serious split among school aid proponents developed again over the religious issue during the 1961 Congressional session. Indeed, the conflict became so intense that one close observer predicted:

> The bitterness of the 1961 legislative struggle and the difficulties of reaching a consensus on the status of nonpublic schools will not soon be forgotten. In private, many school-aid supporters admitted that federal aid of the sort proposed by President Kennedy was dead, not just for the 87th Congress, but probably for the decade of the 1960's.[16]

The Race Issue

Between the debacles of 1949 to 1950 and 1961 over the religious issue, the middle 1950's were characterized by proponent division over federal aid to segregated educational institutions.

---

15 Quoted in Congressional Quarterly Service, *Federal Role in Education*, p. 19.
16 Price, "Race, Religion and the Rules Committee," *op. cit.*, p. 67. The Kennedy Administration proposed a program which excluded aid to private schools, and the supporters of aid to nonpublic schools successfully defeated the program.

The opposition to aid for segregated schools was led by the National Association for the Advancement of Colored People (NAACP). Since 1950, the NAACP, which always supported federal aid to education, has insisted that any aid-to-education program include a stipulation barring federal funds to segregated schools.[17] By assuming this stance, the NAACP encountered two types of opposition. First, the stipulation was opposed by the overwhelming majority of southern congressmen who, of course, were steadfastly committed to preserving racially segregated schools and were unalterably against any aid bill which could be used as an instrument to enforce desegregation. Second, resistance also flowed from such staunch advocates of federal aid as the NEA, the CSSO Council and the AFL-CIO. These groups condemned segregated education, but in their enthusiasm to attract southern support for school-aid bills, they generally opposed any anti-segregation amendments to pending bills. In other words, they were willing to "compromise" on the race issue in exchange for a school aid bill, while the NAACP made it clear that their position was not subject to compromise.[18]

The effect of this issue on blocking aid legislation became particularly apparent in 1956 and again in 1960. On both occasions, Representative Adam Clayton Powell (D., N.Y.) presented anti-segregation amendments to pending school aid bills. In 1956, a school construction bill was foiled on the House floor as 96 Republicans first voted to include the Powell amendment and then joined with southern congressmen to defeat the bill. The Powell amendment was added again in 1960, but a combination of Republicans and southern Democrats was not quite large enough to defeat the bill. The bill was later killed in the House Rules Committee, when three southern Democrats joined the four Republicans on the committee in refusing to authorize a House-Senate conference on the legislation.

Fiscal Issues

The inability among the advocates of school aid to achieve cohesien arose not only from disagreements over race and religion, but also from the diverse views expressed on several fiscal matters. In determining strategies, advocates often differed on the size of the grant that would be "politically acceptable," and on whether or not a grant

---

[17] Prior to 1950, the NAACP had stressed the equal distribution of funds among schools. See Munger and Fenno, *op. cit.*, pp. 65-72.

[18] For an articulation of the NAACP position, see the 1961 testimony of Clarence Mitchell in House Committee on Education and Labor, *Federal Aid to Schools*, p. 666.

program should require matching funds from state and local governments. Disagreements also erupted over whether aid should be distributed in some sort of equalizing fashion or on a flat-grant basis; that is, whether poorer states should receive a relatively larger proportion of proposed federal aid than wealthier states or whether all states should receive an equal amount per pupil regardless of their own resources. Additional proponent discord resulted from disagreements over how federal aid should be spent if it was provided. Some supporters argued that the money should be spent only for school construction, while other insisted that assistance for teachers' salaries should also be included in any aid package.

In summary, then, the advocates of school aid were burdened with fighting the basic issues of the need for federal assistance and the fear of federal control, and were at the same time involved with internal dissension over highly emotional sub-issues: race, religion, and money.

Presidents and Federal School Aid

One student of the federal aid issue has suggested that a necessary ingredient for surmounting such formidable obstacles is the exercise of unusual political leadership by the President. He argues that a basic factor in initiating a breakthrough is a President who is more than merely in favor of federal aid; "the President would have to be for it in a broad and comprehensive way, and feverishly enough to give it a top priority in his program."[19] To what extent has school aid received such attention, and how willing have postwar presidents been to devote substantial amounts of political resources, prestige, and persuasion to the cause of federal aid to education?

President Harry S. Truman was elected in 1949 on a platform that endorsed federal aid to education, and he made it part of his Fair Deal program which was presented to the 81st Congress. A school aid bill did pass the Senate during that Congressional session; however, as we noted earlier, the House deliberations were marred by bitter controversy over aid to parochial schools. Although President Truman did not engage in a major effort to resolve the impasse, the intensity of the conflict makes it doubtful that action on his part would have settled the question. His attention to school aid was necessarily limited because other aspects of his domestic program, such as his compulsory health insurance plan, the establishment of a new executive department of Health, Education, and Security, the repeal of the Taft-Hartley Act, and abolishment of the poll tax, all experienced serious

---

[19] Bendiner, *Obstacle Course on Capitol Hill*, p. 192.

misfortune. Consequently, although President Truman favored federal assistance, his difficulties with his overall domestic program and the heated religious conflict surrounding the federal aid issue during his term afforded him little opportunity to assume a strong leadership role in federal aid to education.

With President Eisenhower's attitude toward school aid (expressed in the letter quoted earlier) and the fact that he was elected on a platform clearly opposing aid to education, it is not surprising that he was opposed to school aid during his first term. But, during his first term, he did propose a White House Conference to study educational problems, particularly the question of federal involvement. The White House Conference on Education began in November, 1955, amid charges that it was stacked by those who opposed federal aid, but its eventual endorsement of the aid muffled critics. Subsequently, the Eisenhower Administration modified its opposition toward aid and proposed a school construction bill in 1956, which, unfortunately for the proponents, became entangled with the segregation issue and was defeated on the House floor. One year later a similar proposal was killed in the House by a vote of 208 to 203 (111 Republicans voted against the bill; 77 voted for it) as both Republicans and Democrats charged President Eisenhower with providing less than enthusiastic backing for his own bill.[20] In sum, it is clear that President Eisenhower was anything but "feverishly" in favor of federal school aid. His original opposition to the policy, his revised "lukewarm" support, and his general budgetary philosophy did not result in a strong presidential effort to initiate such a program.

President Kennedy presented a striking contrast; he made federal aid to education one of the 1960 campaign issues and a key item of his domestic program. His concern with the question is testified to by Theodore Sorensen, who has written that education was "the one domestic subject that mattered most to John Kennedy. . . . Throughout his campaign and throughout his presidency, he devoted more time and talks to this single topic than to any other domestic issue."[21]

Unfortunately for Kennedy, and for the supporters of school aid, he was the first Catholic President. As the second Catholic candidate for the presidency in American history, Kennedy recognized the political necessity of explicitly stating his view on the proper relationship between church and state. Consequently, during the 1960 campaign, he endorsed federal aid on many occasions, but he also stressed that he

---

[20] See Munger and Fenno, *op. cit.*, p. 149.
[21] Sorensen, *Kennedy* (New York: Harper and Row, 1965), p. 358.

favored aid *for public schools only*, and was opposed to providing funds to parochial schools.

It was not surprising, then, that his 1961 legislative program for elementary and secondary education excluded funds for nonpublic schools. This omission triggered strong opposition from Catholic groups, resulting in defeat for the Kennedy aid program. Although requests were repeated in the following years, the intensity of the 1961 fight discouraged both the administration and Congressional proponents from making another major effort. Therefore, although Kennedy was a strong advocate of federal aid, the fact that he was the first Catholic President and that he assumed a firm stance against aid to nonpublic schools during the 1960 campaign seriously restricted his maneuverability on the issue.

The advocates of federal school aid found that, for one reason or another, the three postwar Presidents preceding Lyndon Johnson did not expend substantial political resources in the cause for federal aid. Kennedy was clearly the strongest supporter, but the religious factor proved too arduous. In reference to Kennedy, one writer concluded: "The President was simply not prepared to jeopardize his whole legislative program—and perhaps his chances for re-election—by a bitter fight to the death for aid to education."[22]

Congressional Structure

In addition to all of the above obstacles, the proponents of aid were faced with the fact that the entire institutional structure of Congress is rigged against producing change. The bias against innovation derives from the necessary approval of a new policy by two House Committees; one Senate Committee; both legislative bodies; the House Rules Committee a second time, if a conference is necessary; the President; and finally, if the policy is to be carried out, the Appropriations Committees. On the other hand, the opponents of innovation need block a proposal at only one of these hurdles. With such decentralization of power in the Congressional system, the opponents of federal school aid bills have found the internal institutional structure an important advantage in their efforts to defeat proposed programs.

The impact of these features on school aid legislation was particularly apparent in the House.[23] In that chamber, the proponents were unable for several years to accomplish the most elementary victory,

---

[22] Price, *op. cit.*, p. 68.

[23] The Senate has been much more receptive to federal school aid. Bills were approved in 1948, 1949, 1960, and 1961 before the 1965 enactment.

that is, to muster sufficient strength in the House Education and Labor Committee to have a bill reported favorably. The proponents were usually able to secure committee hearings during the years after World War II; however, it was not until 1955 that a bill finally was reported from the committee. Committee disagreement over the religious issue prevented a favorable report in the late 1940's, and the behavior of the committee chairman, Graham Barden, stalled favorable committee action during much of the 1950's. A southern Democrat from North Carolina, Barden was vigorously opposed to federal school aid, and utilized all of the varied powers of a Congressional Committee chairman to bury school aid proposals before his committee.[24] Barden's ability to obstruct aid legislation was augmented by the characteristics of his committee. The House Education and Labor Committee was considered by many observers the most fiercely partisan and conflict-prone committee in the House. The committee's style of decision-making did not emphasize accommodation and compromise. These features magnified the significance of the ratio of Democrats to Republicans on the committee. In this respect, the sweeping Democratic congressional victory of 1958 and the consequent alteration of the committee's party ratio to produce twenty Democrats to ten Republicans in 1959, instead of the previous ratio of seventeen Democrats to thirteen Republicans, constitutes one of the key institutional changes of the federal aid movement.

In 1959, liberal committee members claimed that in past sessions, the old ratio had allowed an alliance made up of the Republicans, Chairman Barden, and Phil M. Landrum (D., Georgia), to bring about about a 15-15 voting split and thus block action on education aid as well as anti-corruption labor legislation and revisions of the Taft-Hartley Act.[25] This conservative coalition permitted the opponents of federal aid to bottle up proposals at the committee level until 1955; then the Eisenhower Administration presented a program, and the Eisenhower-oriented Republicans on the committee joined the majority of the Democrats to report the bill out. This latter alignment was responsible for reporting bills out in 1956 and 1957, but it was dissolved in 1958 when President Eisenhower withdrew his support for federal aid. Following his withdrawal of support, the old coalition again stalled proposals in the committee. The adoption of a new two-to-one ratio and the appointment of five "liberal" Democratic freshmen in 1959 strengthened the position of committee liberals and gave them

---

24 Munger and Fenno, *op. cit.*, pp. 122-124.
25 *Congressional Quarterly Weekly Report*, January 23, 1959, p. 101.

a dominant majority. Since the alteration in committee size was made and the change from Barden to Adam Clayton Powell as chairman of the committee was accomplished in 1961, the support for federal aid within the committee has been essentially an all-Democratic majority, able to process bills through the committee stage whenever the Administration made earnest requests.

These two alterations unquestionably enhanced the Education Committee's possibilities of securing favorable action on federal aid legislation. Once school aid supporters successfully vaulted that hurdle, however, they were confronted with another barrier: the House Rules Committee, where aid-to-education bills were killed in 1959, 1960 and 1961. The Rules Committee functions in the House as the intervening structure between the committees and the floor. It is charged with the responsibility of determining which committee-approved measures will be debated, and under what conditions. Since 1937, when a group of dissident Democrats joined the conservative Republicans on the committee to oppose much of President Franklin Roosevelt's legislative program, a bipartisan conservative alignment consisting of four Republicans and two Democrats controlled the committee and generally blocked "liberal" legislation. This conservative stronghold was finally broken in 1961, when the House voted to expand the committee membership from 12 to 15, making possible an eight to seven "liberal" majority.

When, by 1961, the Congressional institutional barriers had been overcome, the task remaining for school aid proponents was resolution of the traditional conflicts that had prevented consensus. Three extensive studies of the federal aid issue, completed in the early 1960's, all predicted that such a consensus was unlikely to materialize for at least a decade, but in 1965, Congress approved a bill that has been referred to as the first program of general aid for elementary and secondary education in America's history.[26]

III. The Enactment of ESEA

The passage of the Elementary and Secondary Education Act of 1965 resulted from several interrelated changes rather than from a single, major change. The history of the federal aid issue is clearly partisan, with Democrats generally supporting aid, with varying degrees of intensity depending upon the specifics of a bill, and Republi-

---

[26] The three studies included: Munger and Fenno, *op. cit.*; Price, *op. cit.*; and Bendiner, *op. cit.*

cans generally opposing aid, except for a few years during the Eisenhower Administration. The Democratic landslide in the 1964 election was significant to the fate of school aid legislation in the 89th Congress. The gain of two Democratic Senators reinforced the liberal majority in the Senate, while the increase in the House resulted in the largest number of Democratic representatives (295) and the greatest Democratic plurality (155) since the days of the New Deal. The new Democratic majority in the House was particularly important because it was gained at the expense of Republicans who had previously opposed school aid legislation. Indeed, every one of the forty-eight newly-elected Democrats in the House who filled a seat formerly held by a Republican voted for the ESEA. An equally interesting statistic is that, of the 201 non-southern Democrats voting on the bill, 197 supported it, while a mere four opposed. This margin meant that the proponents needed to gather only twenty-one votes from southern Democrats and/or Republicans to enact the measure in the House, where majorities for federal aid had been most difficult to realize. Given this sizable numerical advantage, the Administration forces were faced with drafting a bill that would not split the large Democratic majority over such perennial issues as segregation, religion, and the allocation of funds.

The chances of preventing such a split over the segregation issue increased with the passage of the Civil Rights Act of 1964. Under Title VI of the Act, no program or activity receiving federal assistance may discriminate against persons because of race, color, or national origin. If a federal agency found such practices to exist, and if they were not voluntarily terminated, the agency was authorized to halt distribution of funds to the unit involved, after providing an opportunity for a hearing and after giving the appropriate legislative committees thirty days notice. This law eliminated the question of aid to segregated schools from the sphere of discussion during the 1965 Congressional hearings and floor debates on aid to education. Undoubtedly, many southern Representatives perceived the Education Act of 1965 as another central government weapon against the traditional southern school system. In spite of the lingering racial question in some minds, however, the bill did receive enough southern support that the Democratic vote alone (228 to 57) was sufficient to gain passage of the bill in the House and in the Senate as well (55 to 4).[27]

In the face of the substantial Democratic majority and the tentative neutralization of the race issue, the memory of the bitter 1961 struggle

[27] *Congressional Quarterly Weekly Report*, April 2, 1965, pp. 600-601, and April 16, 1965, p. 691.

over aid to nonpublic schools remained as the key issue with potential to block school aid in 1965. The outcome of the 1964 election contributed another plus for school aid proponents in the person of Lyndon Johnson. As had his predecessor, President Johnson enthusiastically endorsed an expanded federal role in education, and he made federal aid to education, at all levels of the system, one of the paramount features of the "Great Society." In fact, his interest was so strong that he wanted to become known as the "Education President." Added to this commitment was the fact that Johnson was a non-Catholic, who was not forced to take a hard line on the separation of church and state; thus he had more freedom than had Kennedy for promoting a compromise on assistance to nonpublic schools.

Taking advantage of this latter factor, the President, in the fall of 1964, instructed the Commissioner of Education, Francis Keppel, to prepare an education bill that would avoid earlier struggles over the church-state issue. Keppel and several other Administration officials conducted a series of informal meetings that brought together representatives from the National Catholic Welfare Conference, the National Education Association, the National Conference of Churches, and leaders of the Democratic majority in Congress.[28] The details of the 1965 bill were not hammered out in the meetings, but the meetings did establish what was "acceptable" to the relevant groups and did, for the first time, establish a dialogue between the NCWC and the NEA. That the meetings were successful in stimulating a new consensus became apparent on January 12, 1965, when President Johnson delivered his education message to Congress detailing the content of ESEA. On that day, both the NCWC and the NEA publically endorsed the President's program.

From the President's message and the subsequent legislative draft of ESEA, it became clear that three of the five titles included provisions for assisting both public and nonpublic school students. Under Title I, grants would be allocated to school districts where three per cent of the elementary and secondary students, or a minimum of 100 children, were from families with annual incomes less than $2,000. Funds made available under this provision were to be used to develop programs to meet the special needs of educationally deprived children. In establishing and executing such programs, the local educational agency would be required to consider the number of educationally deprived students attending private schools in the area, and to make

---

[28] Eugene Eidenberg and Roy D. Morey, *An Act of Congress* (New York: W. W. Norton and Co., Inc., 1969), pp. 77-88.

provisions for including special educational services and arrangements (such as dual enrollment, educational radio and television, and mobile educational services and equipment) in which such children could participate. Emphasis was on introducing or increasing, depending on the history of the particular school district, "shared-time" educational experiences in which both public and private school children would be involved. Title II would make available for children's and teachers' use in public and private schools, library resources and other instructional material, including textbooks, to improve educational quality in the schools. Private and parochial school students would also benefit from the provisions of Title III, which called for the establishment of "Supplementary Educational Centers and Services." Under this title, a wide variety of services and educational activities could be provided to all students.[29]

Although the President's program did not furnish direct funds for private and parochial schools (the stress was on aiding *students*, not *institutions*), it did offer them participation in developing some of the programs and made it compulsory that nonpublic school students be given an opportunity to share in the educational program, materials, and services provided under the relevant titles of the legislation. Several groups maintained that these features of the bill violated the principle of separation of church and state; however, continued support from the key groups noted above formed the nucleus of a new proponent coalition that proved sufficient to prevent a serious flare-up and to gain the necessary Congressional approval.

In addition to striking an acceptable compromise on the church-state issue, the 1965 bill was based on a new rationale for federal aid to education. Instead of summoning the same witnesses to reiterate the same statistics showing the existence of an educational crisis revolving around enrollments, classroom shortages, teacher shortages, and meager state-local tax resources, the Administration bill centered on such terms as "the poverty-stricken family," "the poverty cycle," "the disadvantaged student," and "the crisis confronting urban school systems."

In this sense, the rationale used for Title I, the key section of the 1965 bill, was clearly an improvement over earlier proponent arguments. It effectively focused on educational problems that were undisputedly acute. Whereas opponents of federal aid could bring forth reams of statistics, as they had in the past, to "demonstrate" that the classroom and teacher "shortages" were being dealt with adequately

---

[29] Titles IV and V of ESEA supplied federal funds for educational research and for strengthening state education departments.

by state and local resources, they were unable to cast doubt on the seriousness of the educational problems of poverty-stricken students. Ideologically, it was difficult for opponents of federal aid (and such groups as NCWC and the NEA) to be publicly against providing aid that would enable poverty-stricken children to receive an adequate education. Not only did the new rationale weaken the opposition, it also helped to unite the proponents of federal support for education. Aiding disadvantaged students in urban and rural slums was a program that all long-time proponents could back with enthusiasm. Presenting the legislation in these terms averted repetition of past instances in which major supporters disagreed among themselves as to whether aid should be for classroom construction or teachers' salaries or both. The rationale encouraged passage of the bill in still other ways. By utilizing the poverty theme, the education bill probably profited from the political momentum of the overall anti-poverty program. Poverty legislation was a cornerstone laid by the Johnson Administration in its attempt to build the "Great Society." The Economic Opportunity Act was passed in August, 1964, by a Congress which had fewer liberal Democrats than the 89th Congress. Legislation presented in 1965 and linked to poverty would therefore be most attractive to the many congressmen who profited by the Johnson landslide in November of 1964. The poverty formula used in the legislation allocated funds to 95 per cent of the nation's counties, which meant that every congressional district would qualify for some school aid.[30]

The substance of ESEA, then, was politically attractive. An amenable balance was struck on the church-state issue, the shift to the poverty theme in Title I strengthened the proponent argument for federal involvement, and the other titles of the bill contained "a variety of benefits, while denying to each protagonist his full range of demands."[31] One witness before the Education subcommittee articulated the opinion of many commentators when he described the bill as a "fantastically skillful break in the stalemate."

Despite these positive features and the favorable political climate produced by the 1964 election, the administration took no chances with the 1965 bill. History had taught that virtually anything could happen to a school aid proposal. Therefore, they devised a strategy which

---

[30] The bill provided funds to school districts based on the total number of 5- to 17-year-old children in the district from families with annual incomes below $2,000 and from families with higher incomes as a consequence of aid-to-dependent children relief payments multiplied by 50 per cent of the average per-pupil expenditure in the state during the school year 1963-64.

[31] Stephen K. Bailey and Edith R. Mosher, *ESEA: The Office of Education Administers a Law* (Syracuse: Syracuse University Press, 1968), p. 48.

contained some risks, but was fashioned to speed the bill through the Congressional process as rapidly as possible without any alterations that might endanger the delicate coalition of support that had been woven together. Specifically, the plan was to speed the bill through the House, without amendments, in record time and then have the Senate pass the exact same bill so as to avoid the need for a conference.

With only a few exceptions, this strategy was successfully executed.[32] Indeed, the 1965 bill was passed in less than three months, an unusual feat in a policy area of such long-standing conflict. To some extent, this speedy enactment was made possible by the Congressional institutional changes discussed earler and by additional modifications that were accomplished during the 89th Congress. The party ratio on the House Education and Labor Committee, which had been 19 to 12 during the 88th Congress, was a 2-1 Democratic margin (21-10) in the 89th, thus providing the pro-federal aid forces with a clear-cut majority. Swift and favorable action by the committee was also made possible by the fact that Representative Powell, not Barden, chaired the committee and favored both the bill and the Administration's strategy. An expanded Rules Committee, which was permanently established in 1963, and the adoption of a twenty-one-day rule in the 89th Congress, also facilitated a speedy legislative trek for the proposal in the House. The Speaker of the House now had the power to bring a piece of legislation directly to the floor twenty-one days after a standing committee had requested a rule from the Rules Committee, thus reducing the Rules Committee's ability to delay pending action on a bill. And finally, the quick action on ESEA was made possible by the cooperation of Senator Wayne Morse (D. Oregon), chairman of the Education Subcommittee of the Senate Committee on Welfare and Labor, who exercised his talents to pass a bill identical to the House proposal.

From at least two perspectives, the passage of ESEA in 1965 constitutes a watershed in national education policy. First, the legislation is the first general aid-to-education bill enacted by Congress. Second, and more importantly from the perspective of this volume, ESEA represents the major governmental response to the plight of central city students that has been stressed throughout this book. Title I of the

---

[32] The subcommittee of the House Education and Labor Committee changed the provisions under Titles II and III so that *only* public school officials would administer funds instead of the original plan of a partnership between public and private officials. The full committee also accepted the alteration suggested by Representative Roman Pucinski (D., Chicago) to include children in families with incomes over $2,000 derived from welfare payments.

law, which accounted for about $1.1 billion of the approximately $1.3 billion authorized for the fiscal year 1966, was aimed at expanding and improving educational programs "which contribute particularly to meeting the special educational needs of educationally deprived children."[33] In the next section, we will examine the extent to which this goal has been accomplished in the four years since the law was first passed.

IV. The Implementation and Impact of ESEA

Under the Title I provisions of ESEA, local school districts do not automatically receive federal assistance. Federal funds are allocated to state education departments, which distribute the appropriate share of money to local districts only after they have submitted to the state department their plans for establishing and executing programs which:

(1) are designed to meet the special educational needs of educationally deprived children in school attendance areas having high concentrations of children from low-income families and (2) are of sufficient size, scope, and quality to give reasonable promise of substantial progress toward meeting those needs. . . ."

Funding therefore, was linked to reaching the educational needs of low-income students and spending enough money on each student to insure reasonably positive results. Among other provisions, the local districts would evaluate their programs annually and submit reports to state agencies, which also were required to file evaluation reports. In addition, the law directed the President to appoint a twelve-member National Advisory Council on the Education of Disadvantaged Children to review the operation of Title I and report findings and recommendations to the President by March 31 of each year. (This report date was changed to January 31 in 1967).

It is difficult, of course, to assess a large, innovative program that experienced vast administrative problems in its first year and has been in operation for only a few years. Among other things, initial funding did not begin until after the 1965-66 school year had already begun; many state and local educational officials were unfamiliar with the program and lacked experience and personnel for developing compensatory education programs; and the U.S. Office of Education faced

---

[33] U.S. Congress, Senate Committee on Labor and Public Welfare, *Elementary and Secondary Education Act of 1965*, 89th Cong., 1st Session, 1965, p. 25.

numerous problems in establishing program guidelines and dealing with the political problem of "federal control."[34] Evaluation is also complicated by the fact that few school districts had base-line data on low-income students; the educational objectives for such students are unclear; and the tools for measuring educational "progress" are crude.

With these reservations, it is still possible at least to identify initial trends concerning the effectiveness of the program. Although the official published reports do not include much hard empirical data, they project the impression that positive results have not been achieved in most instances, although there are scattered examples of successful programs. After an analysis of 116 projects, the National Advisory Council concluded in 1968 that "the bulk of Title I funds, as represented in the sample, were spent on the intensification of existing approaches to teaching of subject matter. Only a small portion was spent on genuinely new approaches to guiding and stimulating learning."[35] One year later, the Council reported that:

> Owing partly to political pressure and partly to normal human desire to do *something* for as many children as possible, many school administrators have spread their limited funds over very large groups; the average Title I expenditure per child during 1965–66 and 1966–67 was $96 and $99 respectively—hardly enough to make a significant difference. In consequence, while the young beneficiaries might have a hot lunch for the first time, all their other handicaps go untouched, and Title I funds—while spent entirely for worthy purposes—have simply failed to achieve the overall purpose of the legislation.[36]

The Center for Urban Education has conducted independent evaluations of over 60 projects and has arrived at a similar conclusion. "The Center reports document a series of earnest attempts and invite an impression of cumulative failure."[37]

---

[34] For an excellent study of the ESEA implementation process and the problems encountered, see Bailey and Mosher, *op. cit.*

[35] *Third Annual Report of the National Advisory Council on the Education of Disadvantaged Children* (Washington, D.C.: U.S. Government Printing Office, 1968), p. 9.

[36] National Advisory Council on the Education of Disadvantaged Children, *Title I-ESEA: A Review and a Forward Look—1969* (Washington, D.C.: U.S. Government Printing Office, 1969), pp. 14-15.

[37] Robert A. Dentler, "Urban Eyewash: A Review of 'Title I/year II,'" *The Urban Review* (February, 1969), p. 32. Bailey and Mosher, *op. cit.*, also write that: "No state in the union has conducted a more elaborate testing of pupil performance than New York. For the past three years, it has tested annually every first, third, sixth, and ninth grade child in the State in both public and private schools in terms of achieved skills in reading and arithmetic. After two years of ESEA funding, there is no apparent change whatsoever in the performance of children attending Title I-aided schools in low status areas" (pp. 222-223).

The 1969 annual report of the National Advisory Council includes descriptions of successful programs in hopes that they will be emulated in other school districts; however, it is apparent from the other material that the programs included are the few exceptions within a pattern of general failure. The factors which account for this general failure are difficult to determine, but, again, there are some suggestive clues.

The amount of federal resources devoted to the program relative to the magnitude of the problem is an obvious shortcoming. In 1966, the nation had an estimated 15 million educationally disadvantaged children, yet only 7 million such children participated in Title I projects.[38] As the figures in Table 11 indicate, Congress has not made a notable effort to expand the program to reach the universe of disadvantaged

TABLE 11

Authorizations and Appropriations
for Title I of ESEA, 1966-1970
(In millions)

Fiscal Year	Authorized	Appropriated
1966	$1.070	$ .775
1967	1.433	1.070
1968	2.563	1.191
1969	2.725	1.123
1970	2.862	1.010*

* Advanced funding for fiscal 1970
Source: *Congressional Quarterly Almanac, 1965, 1966, 1967 and 1968.*

children. Although fiscal authorizations for Title I have steadily increased, monies actually appropriated have lagged significantly behind. Indeed, between 1968 and 1969, appropriations were cut $68 million, forcing the 1969 program to operate at about 90 per cent of the 1968 program. Unless the advance funding for 1970 is supplemented, the program will be cut an additional $113 million, which would put it at a level below 1967.[39] In addition to this apparent weakening of Congressional commitment, is the point noted earlier that funds provided have been thinly spread by school officials who understandably are

---

[38] *First Annual Report of the National Advisory Commission on the Education of Disadvantaged Children* (Washington, D.C.: U.S. Government Printing Office, 1969), p. 5.

[39] In response to complaints that annual funding caused considerable hardships for local officials, Congress agreed in 1967 to authorize funds for two-year periods.

attempting to reach larger numbers of needy students.[40] As a result, millions of disadvantaged students are not even touched by ESEA and most of those who do participate receive assistance which is less than half of the $200 per-pupil level that professionals judge necessary for conducting a reasonably effective compensatory education program.[41]

More important than inadequate funding is the unproductive utilization of funds by many local school systems. Numerous statements throughout the annual reports of the National Advisory Council indicate that many local districts have used the additional federal funds simply to continue the ineffective practices of the past instead of developing more innovative approaches. Below is a sampling of such findings:

> In some districts money continues to be spent on the expansion of old curricula that are already blind alleys, or on glamorous equipment which local officials deem necessary but which may do little to improve the quality of learning.

> Almost all modern educational theorists agree that young learners, particularly those whose background experiences we classify as disadvantaged, need an abundance of sensory and motor experience dealing with concrete objects before they proceed to abstract learning. . . . Of the 116 projects surveyed, only 35 were reported to using such concrete materials.

> In many schools, more attention is directed to alleviating the symptoms of children's deficiencies than to understanding their causes.

> Major modifications of the curriculum to increase its relevance to the children's lives were recorded in 28 projects—slightly less than one-quarter of all those surveyed.

> . . . One area of almost no apparent progress is the one in which some progress might have produced the most dramatic results of all: Parent involvement in the child's learning. [However,] of the 116 programs observed by the council's consultants, only two gave evidence of any attempt to involve parents as reinforcing agents in their children's learning. . . .

---

[40] It is impossible to note this decline in school expenditures without mentioning the impact of the Vietnam War. Despite the rhetoric of the Johnson Administration concerning "guns *and* butter," it is clear that the domestic budget suffered at the expense of the defense budget. Between 1965 and 1969, defense spending went from a total of $46.2 billion to $77.2 billion, and Vietnam expenditures from $103 million to $26.3 billion. See *Congressional Quarterly Almanac 1968*, p. 748.

[41] Bailey and Mosher, *op. cit.*, p. 117.

Indeed, a reading of the National Advisory Council annual reports uncovers an interesting shift in the thinking of the council regarding the nature of the problem. The first report places heavy emphasis on the shortcomings of "disadvantaged" students (family background, neighborhood environment, low motivation, etc.) and says nothing about the shortcomings of the school system in helping the students to compensate for these disadvantages. The subsequent reports, however, place increasing stress on the shortcomings of many school districts. Although there is an obvious effort not to be overly critical of the schools and to note that they alone cannot be expected to solve the complex problems of the society, the point is made in a variety of ways that many districts have failed to use the new resources competently.

A dramatic illustration of this failure came to light in June, 1969, when the federal government demanded that the Illinois State Superintendent of Schools, Ray Page, return $1.3 million of Title I funds. The demand was based on an audit report which discovered that Page had authorized the use of federal funds to replace regular budgetary needs instead of on programs specially designed for low-income students. For example, money was spent on hiring state officials and buying office equipment that had no relation to Title I; the Chicago Board of Education was permitted to use $412,486 to pay "unwarranted and unreasonable" overtime to principals and janitors; several local school districts spent virtually all their funds on movie equipment; and one school district spent 86 per cent (or $220,591) of its Title I money on equipment and administration.[42]

These findings raise a complex issue. While it is evident that more money will not automatically result in successful compensatory education programs, it is also apparent that worthwhile programs will not come cheaply—substantial fiscal resources are required to meet the needs of poverty-stricken students. There is, therefore, an inclination to devote vast sums of money to improving the quality of ghetto schools, but there is also the realization that many school districts have not used the limited assistance well, and are apt to do the same with additional funds.

The U.S. Office of Education has responded cautiously to this dilemma. Sensitive to accusations of "federal control," the Office of

---

[42] *Chicago Sun-Times,* June 29, 1969, p. 1. According to a recent report by the NAACP Legal Defense and Education Fund, Inc., the Illinois experience is not an isolated case. The report states that a large portion of ESEA money has been "wasted, diverted or otherwise misused by state and local authorities." See *The New York Times,* November 9, 1969.

Education has not sought to link funding to successful efforts. Federal guidelines, of course, have been issued (and re-issued) and local officials have complained about massive "red tape," but Section 604 of ESEA prohibits the Office of Education "to exercise any direction, supervision, or control over the curriculum, program of instruction, administration or personnel of any educational institution or school system. . . ." Consequently, the Office of Education has attempted to encourage more innovative programs by disseminating examples of programs which have met with some measure of success. Whether or not this low-keyed approach will have an impact remains to be seen.

Aside from the traditional resistance to "federal control" and the provisions of Section 604, the Office of Education has also been constrained in implementing ESEA and utilizing it as an innovative force by the furor that has accompanied the Office's enforcement of the 1964 Civil Rights Act. The *Brown* decision of 1954 made possible the filing of individual laws to desegregate specific school districts. Since such lawsuits were time-consuming and expensive, only token desegregation was achieved in the decade following the 1954 decision.

In contrast, the Civil Rights Act of 1964 provided the federal government, for the first time, with several important tools for assuming a major role in desegregating schools. Under the Act, authority was granted to sue, to provide technical and financial assistance, and, most important, to withhold federal funds. Thus, at approximately the same time that the Office of Education was making a major effort to implement ESEA, it was also engaged in the sensitive task of applying the new Civil Rights law to southern school districts.[43]

Enforcement guidelines were first issued early in 1965. The regulations stated that school districts would satisfy the Department of Health, Education, and Welfare requirements if they were under a court order or if they submitted a desegregation plan which was approved by the Commission of Education. Freedom-of-choice plans, in which a student or his parents could choose the school he was to attend, were acceptable under the guidelines. It had become apparent by 1967, however, that freedom-of-choice plans were largely ineffective, so new guidelines were issued in March, 1968, stating that if segregation remained under a free-choice plan, the school system was responsible for taking whatever steps were necessary to achieve desegregation. The fall of 1969 was set as the latest date for bringing

---

[43] For a summary of school desegregation action, see *Congressional Quarterly Weekly Report*, February 14, 1969, pp. 255-261.

about a completely integrated system. As of January 30, 1969, federal funds were cut off from 129 southern school districts, but under the new guidelines, regulations also applied to northern school systems.

Congressional conflict over school desegregation erupted during consideration of the amendments to ESEA in 1966 and 1967. Among the amendments presented by the Administration in 1966 was a provision to grant funds for districts planning school construction to deal with the problems of obsolescence and *de facto* segregation.[44] This provision and the entire relationship between the enforcement of Title VI and the granting of federal school aid was severly attacked on the House floor by both southern and northern congressmen. Commissioner of Education Howe was labeled an "education commissar," "a commissioner of integration," and a "socialist quack." After much heated debate and a House-Senate conference, the ESEA of 1966 was amended to prohibit use of funds for the transportation and for assignment of students or teachers to achieve racial balance. The Office of Education was limited to withholding funds for ninety days unless a hearing was held and a finding of noncompliance was reached.

Passage of the ESEA in 1967 was threatened not only by the school desegregation controversy, but by a Republican move to alter the entire character of Title I by instituting a block-grant approach. Representative Albert H. Quie (R., Minnesota), the third-ranking minority member of the House Education and Labor Committee, proposed that funds allocated under Titles I, II, III and V of ESEA be given in block grants to the states, beginning in fiscal 1969, to be distributed by them according to a statewide plan. The Administration, Catholic groups, Civil Rights groups, and the NEA, among others, vigorously opposed the Quie amendment. Opponents argued that under the proposal, poor students would suffer at the expense of students in wealthier districts and that, since some states have specific laws forbidding aid to parochial schools, the block grant approach would destroy the delicate church-state compromise achieved in 1965 and "create a holy war."

The Quie proposal constituted a serious threat because the 1966 Congressional election results had increased the number of Republican House members from 140 to 187. This shift revived the possibilities of a "conservative coalition" between Republicans and southern Demo-

---

44 Other amendments included: (1) extension of ESEA for four years; (2) reduction of impacted areas funds; (3) repeal of incentive grants for schools which increased expenditures in 1964 and 1965; (4) changing the income level in the formula from $2,000 to $3,000; (5) earmarking additional funds for children of American Indians and migrant workers. See *Congressional Quarterly Almanac, 1966*, pp. 286-297, for a review of 1966 revisions.

crats, as was demonstrated on the first day of the 1967 session when 157 Republicans were joined by 69 southern Democrats to repeal the twenty-one-day rule adopted in 1965. It was obvious to all that the southern Democrats would be in a strong position to determine whether ESEA funds would continue to be allocated according to the poverty formula or on a block-grant basis.

During House debates on the 1967 bill, several amendments were approved which apparently convinced a majority of southern Democrats to stick with their Party's position against the Quie proposal. Congresswoman Edith Green (D., Oregon) introduced an amendment requiring that desegregation guidelines be uniformly applied and enforced throughout the fifty states. The House also accepted an amendment proposed by Representative L. H. Fountain (D., North Carolina) which prohibited the federal government from withholding funds for new programs to schools under Title VI until a hearing had been conducted and the district found guilty of practicing racial discrimination.[45] An amendment presented by Representative Gibbons (D., Florida) was also approved. It provided that the state or national average expenditure per pupil, whichever was higher, could be used in computing Title I funds in fiscal 1968 and 1969. Finally, Representative Green presented two more amendments that were accepted. Both provided greater state control over the provisions of Titles III and V of ESEA. Following adoption of these amendments, the crucial Quie amendment was rejected on a nonrecorded teller vote of 168 to 197. Informal counts of the roll call indicated that the Quie proposal was defeated by lack of southern Democratic support.[46] It was obvious to ESEA proponents that the entire program had survived a very close call.

The combination of the traditional resistance to federal control, the restrictions on the Office of Education contained in Section 604, and the embroilment of ESEA revisions in the politically explosive issue of school desegregation has tended to confine the ability of the federal government to insure that local districts utilize federal funds in a manner that is likely to achieve positive results. The outside force which has the most promise for affecting change in local schools has simply not had a significant impact—low-income students still drop out in greater proportions than other students; they still receive inferior education while in school; and the amount of resources devoted to their schooling still lags seriously behind what is spent on other stu-

---

[45] This amendment was deleted later in the Senate-House conference on the bill.
[46] *Congressional Quarterly Almanac 1967*, p. 611.

dents. The fragmentary evidence that does exist shows that a few school systems have had some success in changing this dismal cycle, but that, on the whole, most systems continue to operate as they have in the past and there is little indication that the federal government, under present circumstances, can effectively alter the situation. Indeed, the possibility exists that sometime in the near future the entire ESEA program may be found unconstitutional. This possibility derives from the fact that several suits have been filed in a number of states challenging the church-state provisions of ESEA.[47] Should these suits be upheld and the program revoked, the entire relationship of the federal government to education would obviously be placed in a confused and unpredictable position.

V. Other "Great Society" Educational Programs

Although ESEA is the major federal educational program especially aimed at improving the educational opportunities of the poor, there is also a wide variety of other programs with the same objective. These programs range all the way from manpower training among the hard core unemployed to preschool programs for three- to four-year-old youngsters.[48] Indeed, one could suggest that the great variety of federal programs contributes to the total problem by encouraging uncoordinated efforts, duplication of activities, rivalries among agencies, and diffusion of scarce money and energy. This situation, however, illustrates well that the federal government and our political system in general tend to respond to problems in a piecemeal fashion rather than with major, radical changes. We will examine briefly three such limited programs—Head Start, the Teacher Corps, and Upward Bound —to illustrate past federal responses and to judge future trends.

The Head Start program was officially announced as part of the federal government's anti-poverty drive in 1965. It was originally intended to enroll 100,000 poor children during the summer of 1965 in 300 communities at a cost of $17 million. But Head Start's popularity encouraged the Office of Economic Opportunity to expand the 1965 program to include 561,000 children in 11,068 centers at a cost of $86 million.[49] Head Start had 473,000 youngsters enrolled in summer programs and 218,000 children in full-year programs by 1968, at a total expenditure of $330 million.

---

[47] Bailey and Mosher, *op. cit.*, pp. 202-203.

[48] For a listing of the major programs, see Francis Keppel, *The Necessary Revolution in American Education* (New York: Harper and Row, 1966), p. 70.

[49] *Congressional Quarterly Almanac, 1965*, p. 410.

During this period, Head Start became the most popular component of the anti-poverty program. Its purpose was to prepare preschool children from low-income, impoverished families for primary school. In addition to basic educational activities geared to giving poor children a better chance to achieve in the regular school system, the Head Start program also included emphasis on health and nutritional services for its clientele. These components were included when it became apparent that many poor children were suffering from physical conditions that would hinder their educational development.

Despite the general popularity of the program and the unusual amount of Congressional support it has received, Head Start has been able to reach only about one-third of the estimated 2.2 million poor children between the ages of three and six. Of those children who are enrolled in Head Start, over two-thirds participate only in the brief summer projects. Federal officials estimate that the cost of supporting a full-year Head Start program for all eligible youngsters would amount to $6.5 billion, a sum greater than the total OEO budget during its first four years.[50] Lack of sufficient funds thus acts as the main constraint on the ability of Head Start to reach the majority of poor children. Another difficulty has been the shortage of personnel with experience in working with low-income children. A national survey of Head Start staff members found that "many staff members received no training at all, despite the fact that more than a third have had no prior experience with preschoolers, and almost half had never before worked with poor children."[51]

Research efforts aimed at evaluating the impact of Head Start have arrived at mixed and inconclusive results. Some early studies found that the program was able to produce significant educational advancements among the preschoolers, while others found no appreciable advance. Some of the follow-up studies concluded that the benefits of the Head Start program had generally faded after the preschoolers had been enrolled in the regular school system for a short period of time, but other studies detected sustained progress. The results of the largest scale study to date (based on a sample of 104 Head Start Centers) were released in April, 1969, and were, with some exceptions, basically negative.[52]

The fundamental question posed by the Westinghouse-Ohio University study was: "To what extent are the children now in the first,

---

[50] Sar A. Levitan, *The Great Society's Poor Law: A New Approach to Poverty* (Baltimore: The Johns Hopkins Press, 1969), p. 140.

[51] *Ibid.*, p. 148.

[52] Westinghouse Learning Corporation and Ohio University, *The Impact of Head Start* (April, 1969). See Chapter One of this study for a comprehensive review of earlier evaluations of Head Start.

second, and third grades who attended Head Start programs different in their intellectual and social-personal development from comparable children who did not attend?" Based on the results of a variety of tests, the study concluded that: "Head Start children could not be said to be *appreciably* different from their peers in the elementary grades who did not attend Head Start in most aspects of cognitive and affective development measured in this study, with the exception of the slight but nonetheless significant superiority of full-year Head Start children on the measures of cognitive development."[53] The study did find, however, that parents of Head Start enrollees were strongly in favor of the program and that there was a great deal of parent participation. One should note that the study did not address itself to such questions as the medical or nutritional impact of Head Start, or its impact on the total community and the schools, or the differences in quality between one Head Start center and another. The results therefore focus on a fairly narrow, but important, dimension of the Head Start program. Nevertheless, the study does add weight to the argument that summer programs are probably too short to have a significant effect and should be replaced by full-year programs that reach children at an early age and continue into the primary grades. Recent developments in the Head Start program have moved in this direction by attempting to enroll younger preschoolers, by shifting to greater emphasis on full-year programs, and by instituting a "Follow-Through" program for graduates of Head Start. Unfortunately, not much has been accomplished in these new directions. President Johnson requested $120 million to support special Follow-Through programs in the primary grades aimed at retaining gains made during Head Start, but Congress granted only $15 million. Therefore, only 4,000 children were reached in 1967-68 and 12,000 during 1968-69, reducing the program to an experiment, when it should have been a broad response to demonstrated need.[54]

In summary, Head Start is one of the most popular of the federal educational programs geared to the special needs of the poor. But, despite its popularity, the program has received funds to reach only one-third of those in need, and of those who are reached, most are involved in brief summer projects which have limited persisting value. Efforts to remedy the major weaknesses of the program and to extend its positive features into the regular school system have been restrained by lack of federal funds. Further, unless the regular school system

---

[53] *Ibid.,* p. 5.
[54] *Congressional Quarterly Almanac, 1967,* p. 1101.

undergoes much reform, there is strong reason to believe that any advances made by Head Start enrollees will be "washed out" in later grades. The long-run impact of Head Start will probably be determined by whether or not it can stimulate the public school system to institute changes that will meet the needs of low-income students. Thus far, there is little evidence to suggest that this is being accomplished.

The National Teacher Corps has not been nearly as popular a program with Congress as has Head Start. The program was first proposed by Senators Edward M. Kennedy (D., Massachusetts) and Gaylord Nelson (D., Wisconsin) in 1965. Kennedy was impressed by the success of trained volunteers who taught black students in Prince Edward County, Virginia, after the public schools had been closed to avoid integration, and Nelson was impressed with the accomplishments of former Peace Corps volunteers who worked as teacher interns in ghetto schools in Washington, D.C. Kennedy's and Nelson's joint proposal called for a two-stage program—a three-month summer training program at a selected college, followed by an in-service work period. Teams composed of an experienced teacher and several young college graduates would be sent into core city or impoverished rural school districts for the in-service work. The goal of the program was to improve the quality of education in poverty areas, but it was also intended to attract idealistic college graduates into the teaching profession and specifically, into schools populated by low-income students.[55]

The proposal was offered as an amendment to the Higher Education Act of 1965, and was quickly endorsed by President Johnson. The Senate approved the amendment immediately, but House Republican conferees refused to sign the Senate-House conference report on the Higher Education Act because of its Teacher Corps provision. They maintained that the program would enable the federal government to exercise unwarranted control over local schools. Nevertheless, the conference bill was approved in both the Senate and the House. It authorized $36 million for fiscal 1966 and $65 million for fiscal 1967 to support the Teacher Corps. During Congressional consideration of the first supplemental appropriations bill for fiscal 1966, however, the Senate voted only $13.2 million for the Teacher Corps, and those funds were eventually deleted in conference because of continued House opposition to the program.

The second supplemental appropriations bill did include $9.5 million for the Corps. House approval was gained by adding two new provi-

---

[55] For a summary history of Congressional action on the Teacher Corps, see *Congressional Quarterly Almanac, 1967*, pp. 418-422.

sions: (1) the bill limited funds to projects specifically approved by state education departments; and (2) the federal government was restricted to paying 90 per cent of the salaries for corpsmen and state or local agencies were required to pay the remaining 10 per cent. The $9.5 million allowed the Corps to recruit members, pay for their training during the summer of 1966, and to place 945 interns and 262 experienced teachers into 275 schools for the 1966–67 school year.

The program ran into greater funding problems in 1967 because the Senate failed to enact the HEW appropriations bill by the time the new fiscal year had begun and the House HEW appropriations bill had deleted all funds for the Corps. A compromise was worked out that allowed the program to continue at the fiscal level of the previous year, but it was prohibited from engaging in any new contracts or commitments to assign personnel to schools until all appropriation bills were enacted. The Corps developed a "temporary procedure" for implementing the in-service phase of the program by having the colleges which were training the Corps members pay the teachers' salaries and the interns' stipends, with the understanding that they would be reimbursed once the funding log-jam was broken. Then, the use of teachers and interns in classrooms generated charges that Corps officials had violated the prohibition of the earlier compromise. This incident led to further funding delays and to Congressional skepticism of the program. As a result of the delays, uncertainties, and conflicts surrounding the program, large numbers left during the training period and many colleges had to cancel their programs.

Despite these drawbacks, the program gained more favorable Congressional support by 1968, but a gap continued to exist between House and Senate backing for the program (reflected in the House's authorization of $15 million and the Senate's $31.2 million for fiscal 1968). The conference compromise of $20.9 million, however, constituted the highest appropriation ever for the program, and represented a stronger commitment to the Corps than had been the case in the past. Senator George Murphy (R., California) spoke in favor of full funding for the program, suggesting the growing Congressional support. Murphy pointed out that he had voted against increasing funds in 1967, but stated "I am now satisfied that the program is doing a good job, and doing it very well."[56] He also pointed out that there were no instances of local school districts' complaining about federal control during implementation of the program.

Although the Teacher Corps was bolstered by Congressional action during 1968, the federal commitment was still far below the original

---

[56] Quoted in *Congressional Quarterly Almanac, 1968*, p. 601.

plans calling for allocation of $65 million for fiscal 1967. Consequently, while the program may be succeeding in introducing a strain of innovation in some schools, it remains only a token program in relation to the magnitude of the problem. As with Head Start, its ultimate impact may be in its ability to stimulate the public school system and teacher training institutions to adopt some relevant changes in teachers' relationships with low-income students.

The Upward Bound program was originally launched during the summer of 1965 through implementation of eighteen pilot projects involving 2,000 students. It was included as a permanent program under the anti-poverty legislation in 1967. The program's objective is to provide high school students from low-income backgrounds and inadequate secondary schools with the skills and motivations necessary to pursue higher education.

Most Upward Bound students enter the program after the tenth or eleventh grade. They attend a six- to eight-week residential summer session on a college campus, followed by sessions during the academic year. Although there is much variation among the programs, the students receive academic training in small groups and in tutorial settings along with programs in athletics, social recreation, and cultural activities. According to follow-up studies, the program has been highly successful in reaching these goals. About 80 per cent of the 5,000 students who graduated from the program in 1967 entered college, and of those, nine out of every ten were still enrolled in college in 1968. Further, the academic record of former Upward Bound students was about the same as other students.[57]

Whether these positive results are due primarily to the quality of the program, the screening out of "high risk" applicants, or the kind of schools attended by Upward Bound graduates, has not yet been carefully analyzed. The fact remains, however, that the program has undoubtedly encouraged some low-income students who probably would not have attended college to do so.

The greatest shortcoming of the program is its scale. The Kerner Report, for example, has estimated that about 600,000 poverty-area students could benefit from Upward Bound; however, the program included only 26,000 students in 1968.[58] In other words, fewer than one out of every twenty students who could profit from the program is being reached. This large gap between need and response is, once again, the result of meager Congressional funding. It would be

---

[57] Levitan, *op. cit.*, p. 171-172.
[58] *Report of the National Advisory Commission on Civil Disorders* (New York: Bantam Books, 1968), p. 452.

necessary for Congress to make a radically larger commitment to both the Upward Bound program and programs which provide financial assistance to low-income college students to move the current situation beyond its token nature.

VI. Conclusions

This chapter reviews the role of the federal government in education. Although the federal government has been involved in education since the beginnings of the nation, general federal assistance for elementary and secondary education, proposed in one fashion or another since 1870, was forestalled until passage of the Elementary and Secondary Education Act of 1965. Although ESEA has been in existence for only four years, early indications are that it has not been successful in improving the quality of education for poverty-stricken students. Estimates indicate that only about half of the 15 million poverty students are involved in Title I programs, and that few of the programs have been successfully executed. This early failure results to some extent from insufficient federal funds, but it is also related to the apparent inability of many school districts to use the funds innovatively.

The potential of the federal government to operate as an innovative force has been constrained by limited Congressional funding and continued resistance to federal involvement in local educational matters. Consequently, although federal involvement in education has expanded greatly during the 1960's, most of the new programs fall far short of demonstrated need. Only the federal government has the fiscal resources to make the magnitude of programs significant, yet there is not sufficient federal commitment to do so. Nor is it clear that the federal government can utilize funds as a means to change state and local educational practices. The level of government that has been most responsive to the special problems of low-income students has failed to realize the goals that were contained in the rhetoric of the "Great Society."

What, then, is the future of urban education? Is there any hope for remedying present conditions or, as some suggest, will the situation become worse before change can occur? These are the questions we turn to in the following chapter.

The Future of Urban Education: Strategy Alternatives and Political Realities

7

I. Introduction

During the 1950's, public attention centered on the linkage between metropolitan change and suburban school districts. Older suburban communities were forced to expand greatly their school facilities to accommodate the school enrollment explosion, and new communities were confronted with the task of building entirely new school systems. Although these goals were eventually realized, they were not achieved without strain and controversy over taxes, curriculum, educational philosophy, and personnel questions. Indeed, as Robert Wood has pointed out: "The program and expenditures of suburban schools are quite likely to engender a brand of active, if not frenzied, political behavior that stands in stark contrast to the more controlled decision-making in other parts of suburban government."[1]

Despite these difficulties, most suburban school districts have functioned and continue to function quite well. High proportions of their student bodies graduate and go on to college, and others secure decent jobs. In terms of output, suburban schools have, on the whole, been successful.

---

[1] Robert Wood, *Suburbia: Its People and Their Politics* (Boston: Houghton Mifflin Company, 1958), p. 186.

Throughout the 1960's, it became evident that this record of general success was not the case for central city school systems. The metropolitan process, by concentrating large numbers of low-income students in central cities and diluting the fiscal strength of cities, highlighted the failure of city school systems to meet the challenge of changing conditions. Their inability to educate successfully the growing black segment of their student population was first exposed during the struggle over desegregation. Formal reports and journalistic accounts documented that in many cities, black students and other minority children were densely concentrated in the oldest schools, with ancient equipment and textbooks, and were taught by the least-qualified teachers who relied on outmoded methodologies and irrelevant curricula. The students fell further and further behind academically the longer they remained in such schools. For the first time, parents and others began to realize how unsuccessful and even damaging the schools were for ghetto children. The seriousness of this failure became obvious as more and more attention focused on education as the best means for breaking the poverty cycle and as the basic tool for preparing ghetto youngsters to compete in a highly technical society.

Realizing that the public schools were not preparing their children for such a world, some parents, civil rights organizations, and others sought to desegregate the schools, assuming that if black students were in schools with white students, they would not be so wholly neglected; they would benefit by being a part of the "superior" education provided for whites. Desegregation proponents found that the majority of white society resisted desegregation. Whites were also concerned about the schools' preparing their children for the changing society, and feared that an influx of black students would downgrade their neighborhood schools and threaten the stability of their neighborhoods. As some whites continued to resist integration and others fled to the security of the suburbs or enrolled their children in private schools, it became clear by the late-1960's that integration held little promise as a means for upgrading the educational opportunities for ghetto students.

Throughout the conflict over desegregation, some school systems experimented with compensatory education programs geared to provide special programs for the "disadvantaged." Evaluations of these programs found little measurable difference in the academic progress of students.[2] Many programs were characterized by scant funds and by educational approaches that had never been successful. Emphasis

---

[2] U.S. Commission on Civil Rights, *Racial Isolation in the Public Schools* (Washington, D.C.: U.S. Government Printing Office, 1967), pp. 115-140.

was on the "disadvantaged" background of the students, with little attention to the shortcomings of traditional school practices and personnel. Most compensatory programs were conducted in segregated schools populated almost entirely by low-income students.

Failure to accomplish desegregation and to execute successful compensatory programs convinced a growing number of people by the late 1960's that the only viable strategy for improving the educational progress of ghetto pupils would be to gain community control of the schools. The basic assumption behind this apporach was that the schools would improve their performance if mechanisms were developed to make them more accountable to the community. The primary mechanism would be the establishment of neighborhood school boards composed of parents, community organization representatives, some professional educators, and university representatives. Ideally, the board would have control over the budget, personnel, school plant, and curriculum. Under such a plan, parents and other community representatives would be involved in basic policy-making and, although they would not run the schools on a day-to-day basis, they would be in a position to review the professionals' and para-professionals' performances and to institute necessary changes. Our earlier account of the effort to achieve community control in New York City reveals the intense conflict such efforts are likely to generate in other cities. The proponents of community control, like earlier educational reformers, face a long, uphill struggle.

Although reformers were generally unsuccessful in reaching their goals, they did touch off trends that have changed the nature of school governance. Some of the very things that professional educators fear most have occurred as a by-product of the recent reform efforts. First, the schools have become entangled in unprecedented controversy. As a consequence, schoolmen in cities have found that it is no longer possible to run the schools in a non-conflict atmosphere or to project a believable image of expert consensus. The insulating walls that surrounded city school systems for decades have been broken down. Public scrutiny and disclosures of the inner workings of the system have exposed widespread failure. These public exposures have stimulated a broadside attack on the professional qualifications and expertise of educators who run the schools. Great pressure has been exerted to break the monopoly of decision-making power that key actors possessed in the past. A growing number of actors currently have at least *indirect* influence on the course of school policy-making, and are making a strong push to secure direct power. The combination of these trends has resulted in a serious undermining of the legitimacy of the school system. A growing number of ghetto parents and organizations no longer have any confidence (if they ever did) in the ability of schoolmen to run the schools successfully. Today's educators are in a vulnerable defensive position, and their control of the operation of schools in the decade ahead is threatened as it has never been in the past.

Despite all of these changes, however, the basic output of urban school systems has not been measurably improved. The schools still do not equip most low-income students to compete successfully in the outside world. Each year a new crop of ghetto children are brought into the system under essentially the same conditions and with essentially the same prospects of achievement as earlier groups. Even those who have benefited from programs such as Head Start begin to fall behind standard levels after a year or so in the regular public school system. Token changes have been accomplished, but none which fundamentally alter the opportunity prospects for most low-income students.

At the local level, most school systems have resisted all meaningful reforms, and even those which have made a major attempt to break with the past, such as Philadelphia, have discovered that administrative reform does not automatically translate into substantive changes.[3] There are virtually no indications that the states will act as catalysts for reform. The states thus far have done little beyond accentuating the disparities by allocating more aid to suburban schools than to city schools. Only at the federal level have programs been enacted which at least move in the right direction. The Education Act of 1965, the Teacher Corps, Head Start, Upward Bound and other programs contain some promise for improving the situation. Unfortunately, however, the results of the Head Start program have been spotty; funding for all innovative programs has lagged far behind demonstrated needs; and the federal government has been restrained from using such programs as levers for instituting meaningful change at the local level.

Given these facts and trends, what is the future of low-income urban students? Are they doomed to the fate of their immediate predecessors or are there strategies for change which have reasonable chances of political success? We will examine several of the major strategies that have been widely discussed, and will assess their political feasibility. These strategies are usually viewed in one combination or another;

---

[3] For an account of the Philadelphia experience, see Wallace Roberts, "Can Urban Schools be Reformed?" *Saturday Review* (May 17, 1969), pp. 70-72; Marilyn Gittell and T. Edward Hollander, *Six Urban School Districts* (New York: Praeger, 1968), pp. 24-50; and Henry S. Resnik, "The Shedd Revolution: A Philadelphia Story," *The Urban Review* (January, 1969), pp. 20-25.

however, we will treat them separately to make the analysis more manageable. We will also formulate some predictions about the future of urban education in the coming decade.

II. Integration

The results of attempting to eradicate *de facto* segregation in northern school districts have varied according to the size of the community involved and the proportion of black students in the school system. Those communities which have implemented reasonably successful integration programs, such as Berkeley, California; Teaneck, New Jersey; Evanston, Illinois; and Champaign-Urbana, Illinois are usually middle-sized communities with a smaller proportion of black students than is generally found in large cities. In contrast, not a single large city has successfully integrated its schools or reversed the trend toward greater segregation. The combination of black population growth, continued white resistance, and withdrawal of white students to private schools and suburbia has worked to defeat integration efforts in the past and will make the possibilities of future integration even more remote. Many large cities will be unable to integrate their public schools because they simply will not have enough white pupils. That kind of situation would necessitate consolidation with suburban districts. The prospects of achieving city-suburban consolidation are so slight that many favor advocates of integration have abandoned it as an unrealistic strategy.

There continue to exist, however, some strong advocates for integrated education. The current proponents cling to the integration strategy for two reasons. First, they point to the findings of the Coleman study which identified the social class milieu of a classroom as the most important "in-school" variable affecting student achievement.[4] The higher the social class background of all students in a particular school, the higher the achievement of an individual student is likely to be, regardless of his own social background. This relationship was interpreted to be particularly important for low-income students, but it has less impact on other students. In other words, low-income students benefit from a middle-class school environment, whereas middle-class pupils tend to achieve at standard levels regardless of the environment. Since blacks as a group lack a sizable middle-class, some maintain that integration is necessary to creating a social

---

[4] *Equality of Educational Opportunity* (Washington, D.C.: Office of Education, 1967).

class environment that will be conducive to advancing the blacks'
educational progress. Integration is thus viewed as a necessary means
to improving achievement among black youngsters, and one which
has no detrimental educational effects on white children.

Some proponents base their arguments for integration on broader
social grounds. They point to the finding of the Kerner Commission
Report that: "Our nation is moving toward two societies, one black,
one white—separate and unequal" and reason that segregated schools
feed this process and thus add to the racial strife of the nation.[5] A
resolution to the racial crisis, it is argued, cannot be accomplished if
black and white children are educated in isolation from one another.
Within this context, Thomas Pettigrew has called attention to the
finding (in *Racial Isolation of the Public Schools*) that both black and
white adults who had experienced interracial schooling during their
childhood were more favorable toward integrated situations, for themselves and their children, than were adults who had not.[6]

From both educational and broad social perspectives, then, school
integration is viewed as an attractive and important objective. Current
political realities, however, indicate that integration for large city
school systems will certainly not be accomplished during the 1970's.
In addition to the obstacles mentioned is the fact that the vanguard of
black leadership has generally rejected (at least for the near future)
the goal of integration in favor of gaining control of institutions that
affect the lives of blacks. Their objective is to attain "black power,"
which will put them in a more powerfully competitive position in our
pluralistic society. In this respect, the contemporary call for integration,
by either blacks or whites, is viewed as a ploy for undermining the
thrust for black power.

With these forces operating at the local level to block integration,
advocates have looked to the state and federal governments to lead
the struggle. Although fourteen states have agencies within their
Departments of Education to deal with the problem of racial balance,
there is no evidence that any of the states have taken or are about
to take the radical steps necessary to accomplish integration. Therefore,
while the states have the power to achieve integration by ordering
the redrawing of school district lines on a metropolitan-wide basis, it
is extremely doubtful that they will do so, considering the growing
political power of suburban representatives.

---

[5] *Report of the National Advisory Commission on Civil Disorders* (New York:
Bantam Books, 1968), p. 1.

[6] Thomas Pettigrew, "School Integration in Current Perspective," *The Urban
Review* (January, 1969), p. 5.

Under the Johnson Administration, the federal government began to utilize Title VI of the 1964 Civil Rights Act to push desegregation in the South and North. (In 1969 South Holland, Illinois, became the first northern district to have funds suspended.) Action along these lines by the Office of Education, as we noted in the preceding chapter, was vehemently attacked by southern and northern congressmen. As a result, the question of enforcing desegregation guidelines (which called for full integration by the fall of 1969) became an issue in the 1968 presidential campaign. Candidate Richard Nixon implied on several occasions that, if elected, he would slow down enforcement, and stated that withholding federal funds to enforce desegregation was "a very dangerous" doctrine.[7] In July, 1969, after much behind-the-scenes negotiation, President Nixon fulfilled his campaign pledge when his Secretary of Health, Education and Welfare, Robert Finch, and his Attorney General, John N. Mitchell, announced jointly that: "It is not our purpose here to lay down a single arbitrary date by which the desegregation process should be completed in all districts, or to lay down a single, arbitrary system by which it should be achieved."[8] Although the statement went on to point out that the "terminal date" for compliance would be the 1969-70 school year, it also held that: "In some districts there may be sound reasons for some limited delay."

Critics of the administration's position pointed out that many southern districts had already delayed desegregation for fifteen years, and that the ambiguous language of the new guidelines invited further delays. On the ambiguity of the new policy, Jerris Leonard, Assistant Attorney General for Civil Rights, stated: "I can't in my wildest dreams tell you how to read it."[9]

This blow to integration, in conjunction with the other factors, leads unquestionably to the conclusion that integration is not a politically realistic strategy. If some degree of integrated education is achieved, it is most likely to occur in middle-sized communities where blacks are not overwhelmingly lower-class and their proportion of the school population is not generally over 20-25 per cent, or in token city-suburban programs where a small number of "select" city black students are allowed to attend suburban schools. Therefore, any reasonable strategy for improving the quality of education for the great bulk of ghetto students must accept segregation, at least for the time being, as a fact.

---

[7] *Congressional Quarterly Weekly Report*, February 14, 1969, p. 261.
[8] "President Eases School Deadline on Desegregation," *New York Times*, July 4, 1969, p. 1.
[9] *Ibid.*

III. Compensatory Education

The strategy of compensatory education has been widely utilized within a segregated framework in the past and will undoubtedly be continued in the future. This approach assumes that the culture of poverty constitutes the major cause of academic failure among minority group children and that the school system must institute special educational programs to overcome the detrimental effects of poverty in the home and neighborhood environment. Title I of ESEA, the Great Cities School Improvement Program, and New York City's famous More Effective Schools Program, are among the more widely-known examples of this approach. Such programs generally stress some combination of remedial instruction, cultural enrichment, ego development, parent involvement, and preschool education.

Although much rhetoric usually surrounds the inauguration and execution of these programs, creating a widespread public image that they are highly successful, empirical evaluations show that they have usually failed to upgrade the performance of low-income students. This failure is normally attributed to the level of funding, the character of the programs, or both.

Critics who stress the funding dimension often focus on city-suburban expenditure disparities as an index. They argue that most special educational programs, which reach only a small fraction of all "disadvantaged" students, generally do not raise expenditures to an amount equal to the outlay for suburban students with strong educational backgrounds. Given the greater needs of city students, they maintain that even parity with suburban expenditures would probably not be sufficient; city schools should spend *more* per pupil than suburban schools if real equality of opportunity is to be offered.

To this writer, the political feasibility of, first, halting the growing gap between city and suburban school expenditures and, then, reaching equality or actually reversing the gap in favor of the cities seems slight. There is little indication that the cities' relative fiscal strength will measurably improve in the decade ahead. Therefore, any substantial increase in school funds would necessarily have to originate from state and federal sources.

With population and thus state political power, constantly shifting toward the suburbs, it is doubtful that suburban state legislators and rural legislators will be particularly interested in allocating more funds to city districts than to their own districts. Further, although state-raised revenue has grown rapidly in recent years, there is constant pressure (and in some states constitutional restrictions) to keep taxes down so that each state may remain in a favorably competitive position to attract industry. While state school aid will obviously increase in the future, there is little evidence that the amount of increase or, more importantly, the city-suburban distribution, will be responsive to the special needs of city schools.

The federal tax structure is more responsive to economic growth than either local or state structures; thus, the federal government alone has access to the massive funds required to support meaningful compensatory education programs. Although the federal government has generally followed an equalization policy in allocating much of its school aid, the level of funding was stagnant during the Johnson Administration. The early "Great Society" predictions of a massive assault on poverty, unemployment, inferior educational opportunities, and so forth, simply did not materialize, as more and more of the nation's resources were poured into the Vietnam War. The first six months of the Nixon Administration provided no hint that large sums of additional federal aid would be poured into the cities. Indeed, such urban-oriented programs as the Job Corps and Model Cities suffered budgetary cuts. Consequently, a greatly expanded commitment to compensatory education at the federal level appears highly unlikely.

Even if large sums of money were made available to city schools, there would still remain the serious question of the local districts' ability to employ additional funds fruitfully. An educator with considerable experience in compensatory education describes it as:

> . . . essentially an additive, or 'band-aid,' approach that works by augmenting and strengthening existing programs. It builds layers onto the standard educational process in order to bring the strays into the fold and to fit them into the existing school mold. The assumption is that the schools need to do somewhat more for the disadvantaged pupils, but it does not presume that the school itself is in need of wholesale re-examination.[10]

According to this perspective, adequately financed compensatory education programs must be accompanied by major school-system reforms to be successful. New teaching methods, new curricula material, new teaching and administrative personnel, a sharp reduction in teacher-pupil ratios, and parental involvement are some of the changes

---

[10] Mario D. Fantani, "Implementing Equal Educational Opportunity," *Harvard Educational Review* (Winter, 1968), p. 164.

necessary to make the compensatory approach effective. Early evaluations of ESEA suggest that instituting such changes within the present
educational system is easier said than done.

From both monetary and substantive perspectives, then, the compensatory education strategy does not appear promising. It is not
likely that massive resources will be allocated to support such programs and, if they were, the present educational system would probably not use them well. Some critics also maintain that inherent in the
compensatory approach is the basic flaw of perpetuating segregated
education. As such, it fails to achieve the social class mixture that the
Coleman Report found to be so important, and it makes it extremely
difficult for white legislators to support programs which favor segregated blacks over their own white constituencies.[11]

IV. Administrative Reform

The avalanche of criticism leveled against the public school system
has not been totally ineffective in stimulating some moderate reforms.
Numerous districts have attempted to remedy some of the more
blatant practices and a few systems, such as Philadelphia, have made
a major effort to accomplish what might be referred to as administrative reform.

Under the leadership of a new board of education, the Philadelphia
system recruited a new, dynamic superintendent, doubled its school
budget in four years, became eligible for more federal school aid per
child than any other large city, and began a $500 million building
program that opens fifteen new schools a year. The new superintendent,
Mark Shedd, launched a wide range of innovative programs, ranging
all the way from introducing "planning, programing, budgeting systems" to hiring a former street gang to direct an orientation program
for new teachers. Despite all this activity, a close observer of the
Philadelphia scene has written that:

> . . . the Philadelphia public school system remains essentially the
> same institution it was before the new regime. The tone is different,
> and a monumental effort at change is in process. . . . But the faults that
> Philadelphia shares with other city school systems are far from being
> totally eliminated.[12]

---

[11] David K. Cohen, "Policy for the Public Schools: Compensation and Integration," *Harvard Educational Review* (Winter, 1968), pp. 129-137.
[12] Henry S. Resnick, "The Shedd Revolution," *op. cit.*, pp. 24-25.

There are two important barriers to meaningful change in Philadelphia. Resnick identifies the "system's pathological commitment to the status quo" as the greatest obstacle to innovation. Administrators, principals, and teachers with many years tenure within the system have been a "formidable and possibly devastating enemy."[13] After long years of working their way up the system's career ladder, these educators are intensely resistant to any innovation, such as a merit-pay system, that would alter the "rules of the game" and possibly put them at a disadvantage. And the resources available to them for preventing change are legion.

Meaningful innovation has also been diluted by the fact that all of the new directions emanate from central headquarters. This has occurred during a period when community groups are becoming more and more distrustful of the "establishment," regardless of whether it is an old or new regime. When new programs devised by "downtown professional educators" fail to produce quick results, community cynicism toward the system increases. This distrust has apparently been intensified in Philadelphia by the failure to achieve community involvement in the decision-making process. For example, efforts by a group of citizens in the Germantown section of the city to gain some control over a new school in the area were fought off by the central administration and the frequent talk of decentralization boiled down to some administrative decentralization, not community control.

Philadelphia's experience strengthens the position of those who maintain that only a radical reform of the public school system will resolve the urban education crisis. They view administrative reform as another "band-aid" approach which does little more than perpetuate an incompetent system. They offer community control and/or competing schools systems as workable alternative strategies.

V. Community Control

In contrast to the preceding approaches, the community control strategy stresses a fundamental redistribution of power. Its premise is that the present system is incapable of reforming itself; progress can be achieved only if decision-making power is located in the hands of those who have a direct stake in the educational achievement of ghetto youth—their parents and the community-at-large. This does not imply that community residents would actually run the schools. Rather, it is

---

[13] *Ibid.*

an effort to strike some balance (at this point undefined) between professional operation of the schools and citizen involvement in policy-making. With control over the budget, personnel, curriculum, and school plant, community school boards would supposedly be in a strong position to create an environment that encourages flexible and innovative approaches to education; one that spurs professionals to develop unorthodox methods for producing positive educational results and one that reduces the community's alienation from the schools. The vision is to make the schools an integral part of the community; to make them institutions which the populace can feel are real opportunity structures rather than symbols of a repressive larger society.

There are many political obstacles to achieving community control. Opponents of community control argue that it would undermine professional educational standards, cause the schools to revert to a patronage system, encourage stifling parochialism, put technical decisions in the hands of untrained laymen, and perpetuate segregated education. Some people who formerly resisted integration now use it as an argument against decentralization. But, some long-term integrationists oppose community control on the grounds that it is a "cop-out" strategy which takes white society "off the hook" and plays into the hands of racists by forcing ghetto residents to carry the responsibility for solving the problem. A combination of all these points has been used to predict that community control would lead to even further decline in the quality of education for low-income students.

Behind the anti-decentralization rhetoric lies, of course, the political power of the opponents. In the New York City case, which is thus far the only well-documented illustration, a coalition of the teachers' union, the supervisors' association, the central administration, the central board, and the allies of these groups, both locally and at the state level, defeated the proponents of community control. Whether a similar outcome will result in other cities is difficult to predict at this time. Perhaps most important among a variety of complex variables is the posture assumed by the teachers, who seem to occupy, at the moment, a swing position. If teacher organizations continue to ally with "the establishment" (and there are strong pressures for them to do so), the opponents will constitute a formidable barrier. On the other hand, if teacher organizations in some cities side with community groups, as they apparently have in Washington, D.C., then the possibilities of achieving greater community control will increase. This pattern is more likely to occur in cities where the teaching staff contains a significant proportion of minority group members.

On balance, however, the odds are against accomplishing widespread community control in the near future. The protectors of the *status quo* are deeply entrenched, and the proponents, although they will continue to push for change, simply lack the political muscle necessary to effect radical change in the present situation. The current holders of power are likely to respond to future pressure by granting minor concessions, such as providing greater involvement for citizen advisory groups and creating some administrative decentralization, but they will jealously guard the real levers of power. Whether they will successfully fend off the thrust for community control is a basic question in the decade ahead.

Although the structural aspects of community control may not be accomplished, it is possible that the substantive objectives will be reached in some cities during the next decade. In Gary, East St. Louis, Newark, Baltimore, St. Louis, Cleveland, and Detroit, blacks will constitute a majority of the population, and will thus be in a *potential* position to gain full control of the school systems. Such has been the case in Gary, for example, where a black mayor, Richard Hatcher, was elected in 1967. Once elected, Hatcher made a series of appointments to the school board (members are not elected) and to a citizens' advisory committee, providing blacks with majority control. As a result, the current board has felt only moderate pressure to decentralize the system. Whether a black-controlled school system will accomplish the objectives of community-control reformers remains to be seen. One of the important constraints it faces, as would community controlled districts in any city, is the local board's heavy reliance on intergovernmental school aid to help support the innovative educational programs desired.

VI. Competing School Systems: The "Free Market" Strategy

Another proposed radical strategy for improving ghetto education is the competitive school system model.[14] The basis of this approach is that an important contributor to the current failure of the public school system and a significant barrier to future reform is the monopolistic hold that public schools have on the educational system. Jencks has argued that if big city schools did not have a monopoly on educational opportunities for the poor and were compelled to compete with

---

[14] Variations of this approach can be found in: Milton Friedman, "The Role of Government in Education," in Robert A. Solo (ed.), *Economics and the Public Interest* (New Jersey: Rutgers University Press, 1955), pp. 124-125; Christopher Jencks, "Is the Public School Obsolete?" *The Public Interest* (Winter 1966), pp. 18-28; Milton Friedman, "A Free Market in Education," *The Public Interest* (Spring, 1966), p. 107; and Kenneth B. Clark, "Alternative Public School Systems," *Harvard Educational Review* (Winter, 1968), pp. 100-113.

private schools, they would probably be forced out of business. Similarly, Clark has argued that:

> What is most important in understanding the ability of the educational establishment to resist change is the fact that public school systems are protected public monopolies with only minimal competition from private and parochial schools. . . . As long as local school systems can be assured of state aid and increasing federal aid without the accountability which inevitably comes with aggressive competition, it would be sentimental, wishful thinking to expect any significant increase in the efficiency of our public schools.[15]

Several methods have been suggested for breaking the monopolistic hold of the public school system. Friedman and Jencks recommend a voucher system to distribute funds for financing education. Under this system, families would be given tuition grants, equal to what is spent per pupil in the public schools, to be spent on purchasing an education in an "approved" private institution. Creation of such a grant system would supposedly stimulate the establishment of highly competitive private schools that would vie with one another to develop a "superior product" and thus attract students. Jencks also suggests that school boards could contract with various organizations (universities, business corporations, churches, etc.) to manage particular schools within the system. Contracts would be renewable on the basis of evaluations. Clark has proposed a variety of quasi-public-private schools, such as regional state schools, regional federal schools, industrial schools, labor union schools, and even army schools.

It is argued that enacting such proposals would foster "diversity, experimentation, and improvement in the quality of schooling." Competition would encourage development of improved educational opportunities for both the poor and non-poor. Under the tuition system, the poor would have "money power"; they would be in a position to bargain with the school system instead of being victimized by it. They would have educational choices that are currently available only to the wealthy. Friedman also maintains that the voucher system would lead to a larger total expenditure for education, since some parents would purchase higher cost schooling by supplementing the standard government grant.

In a recent critique of this strategy, Henry M. Levin suggests that very mixed results would probably occur.[16] He agrees that the strategy would result in some private benefits. Parents would have a greater

---

15 *Ibid.*, p. 111.

16 Henry M. Levin, "The Failure of the Public Schools and the Free Market Remedy," *The Urban Review* (June, 1968), pp. 32-37.

choice among schools and schools would probably improve in order to survive within the competitive framework. The combination of consumer choice and competition among schools would probably lead to a higher quality of education for students than is currently provided by the monopolistic system. Levin cautions against a strictly free-market approach, however, on the grounds that it would widen social disparities rather than equalize educational opportunities for all races and classes. He notes that the market proposal makes no provision for encouraging students to attend racially and socially mixed schools. In fact, the private school record suggests that even greater racial and soical segregation would result than that which we presently have. Not only would greater stratification occur, but the private market would probably provide a greater range of choices and higher quality of education for middle-class children than it would for the poor. Levin maintains that few agencies would choose to provide educational services to the poor since costs would be higher in the ghetto, the job would be more difficult, and middle-class parents elsewhere could afford to supplement the tuition grants and thus attract agencies to their areas. The schools which did serve the poor would find it difficult, for example, to attract the "better" teachers, since most would prefer to teach in middle-class schools for more money. The case of Prince Edward County, Virginia, which abolished its public schools in 1959 and provided tuition grants to all students, as a way to defy the Supreme Court desegregation order, is used to illustrate what might develop under such a system. In that instance, private schools were established to serve white students, but no private schools emerged for black children. Levin argues that "rather than schooling being utilized as a device for equalizing opportunity, the market would enable it to widen the present disparity between the opportunities afforded the privileged and the disadvantaged."

Some modifications in the general approach have been proposed to overcome these shortcomings. One alternative scheme is to provide tuition payments that are inversely proportionate to family income—poor families would be given vouchers worth two or three times the value of grants allotted to other families. Another approach would provide tuition grants only for the poor, giving them the opportunity to choose between ghetto public schools and private institutions. This method would give low-income parents some alternative selections and would encourage at least minimal competition while not increasing educational disparities between the poor and others.

All the variations of the free market strategy face many political obstacles. First, there is the complex constitutional question of providing public funds, even indirectly, to private institutions. Title I of

ESEA was approved by Congress on the grounds that funds were being provided to nonpublic school students, not to the schools themselves (the child-benefit theory), but this practice is currently being challenged in the courts. If it is eventaully upheld, there would still remain the question of governmental regulation. Would tuition grants be usable only at "approved" schools and, if so, what criteria would be used to approve schools? Would government regulation of the "approved" schools force the agencies back into the regimented procedures of the present system? Or would the agencies have sufficient freedom to run schools in a manner inimical to a professed egalitarian and democratic society? These and other equally knotty questions weigh against the adoption of such proposals. Further, the present public school establishment would obviously exercise its full political resources in combatting any major movement that might threaten the very existence of the public school system. Would, for example, the teacher unions in New York, Chicago, or San Francisco, continue to work while the system shifted from public to private control, thereby eliminating teacher-tenure protections? It is highly unlikely that reformers who seek to eliminate the public school system would succeed in a political contest with the educational establishment. Consequently, any major future effort to improve the quality of inner-city education will probably have to be conducted within the public school framework. This does not exclude the possibility of supplementary educational programs conducted by private agencies. Some Head Start schools and Job Corp Centers are run by private agencies, as are southern Freedom Schools. Such schools can, and perhaps will, serve as competitive models for public schools and will encourage them to emulate successful programs. However, the overwhelming proportion of poor students will no doubt continue to be educated in public schools, and it is toward public schools that future reform measures should be directed.

VII. Conclusion: A Decade of Black Emergence?

Within the context of discussing the future options available to American society, the Kerner Commission Report identified three basic educational choices: (1) providing black students with inferior education in racially segregated school systems; (2) providing them with quality education in enriched segregated schools; and (3) providing black students with quality education in integrated schools.[17]

---

[17] *Op. cit.*, Chapter 16, "The Future of the Cities," pp. 389-409.

The foregoing discussion argues that the last alternative, while perhaps the most attractive, is the one least likely to be realized during the coming decade. All of the trends we have discussed point to an increase in segregated education in large cities. Unless a dramatic, unforeseen reversal of these trends emerges, the overwhelming majority of black students will continue to be educated in segregated schools. Consequently, in terms of political realities, the future choices suggested by the Kerner Report are reduced to inferior, segregated education or quality, segregated education in our large cities. Mere continuation or token modification of present structures and policies will generally result in the former choice.

While there is great momentum toward continuance of inferior, segregated education for blacks, there are also some trends that may avert such a future. Among these trends is the continuing flight of whites from core cities and the subsequent increase in proportions of black populations; the growing acceptance of black power ideology in black communities, particularly among the young blacks who will constitute an important political force of the future; and the emergence of black professionals as a political force in northern school systems.

The most recent population reports indicate that, while blacks have continued to migrate into central cities, they have done so at a lower rate than between 1960 and 1966, when black population in central cities grew at an average of 370,000 per year. From 1966 to 1968, black city population growth dropped to about 100,000 per year. During these same periods, however, white out-migration increased from an average of 140,000 a year to almost 500,000 per year.[18] The net result of these demographic shifts will be an even more rapid growth in total black population and black school population in cities than was the case in the early 1960's.

Complementing this demographic fact, and building upon it, is the growing surge of black power ideology in black communities. Although the concept has various meanings, the dimension which concerns black control of community institutions is apparently widely accepted among new leaders. A recent nationwide public opinion study of black people and leaders concluded that:

> Despite the differences in emphasis—and vocabulary—the younger leaders are in accord on many issues. The fundamental one at the moment is what they see as the necessity for blacks to gain increasing control of the ghettos and their institutions—especially the schools and the police. . . . Whether community control is as effective a social tool

---

[18] Urban America, Inc., and The Urban Coalition, *One Year Later* (New York: Frederick A. Praeger, 1969), pp. 110-113.

as its proponents maintain is debatable. But there is no arguing with its pervasive hold on the black leadership today.[19]

The combination of demographic changes, the convergence of black leaders on community control as a primary goal, and the envisioned growth of political organization within black communities to gain control, should enhance the strength of community control advocates. Their position may be enhanced even further by the continuance of black militancy on the part of black high school students. In recent years, such students have engaged in a variety of protest actions aimed at making the schools more relevant to black needs and an instrument of liberation for the black community. This kind of student action contributes to a political context that will keep the present school rulers on the defense, and will provide community control proponents with a significant "in school" ally.[20]

Undoubtedly, the "educational establishment" will continue to exercise its considerable power to frustrate the thrust toward community control and, if teacher organizations remain with the establishment, will probably be successful during the next few years. However (and this is the third significant trend), as teacher organizations in cities become populated by an increasing number of black professional educators, the unions may eventually break with the establishment coalition and join community control advocates in a new alliance. That alliance could force significant changes in who governs city schools and who benefits from the schools. In those cities where such an alliance is forged, it is possible that community control proponents will successfully wrestle power away from the present establishment. In other cities, such as East St. Louis, Illinois, and Gary, Indiana, the entire school system will be run by black educators and local neighborhood control of schools may not be a major issue.

If blacks do gain control of the school system in some cities, it does not automatically follow that educational achievement among black students will suddenly improve. The successful attainment of black control will resolve the problem of legitimacy (that is, who has the legitimate authority to run black populated schools—blacks or whites?) but whether it can resolve the problem of low achievement is another question.[21] The emergence of black control, in either a decentralized

---

[19] "Report from Black America," *Newsweek* (June 30, 1969), p. 25.

[20] On the development of high school militancy, see: Jerome H. Skolnick, *The Politics of Protest* (New York: Ballantine Books, 1969), pp. 162-171.

[21] For a thoughtful discussion of the authority question, see David K. Cohen, "The Price of Community Control," *Commentary* (July, 1969), pp. 23-32.

or centralized fashion, will alleviate many of the characteristics of incompetence in the present public school system and will create a new environment for learning. Significant problems will continue to persist, though; among them, the lack of fiscal resources. Blacks may secure control of some city school systems, but in an important sense, they will be saddled with a costly institution that cannot be supported by local resources. Consequently, the quality of black controlled education, if control is achieved, will be strongly influenced by the political ability of black communities to acquire substantial amounts of intergovernmental revenue for both educational and non-educational programs. Success will be largely determined by whether black communities gain greater representation in state legislatures and Congress, and if the increased number of black legislators operate as cohesive voting blocs which, in turn, will allow them to play the "swing role" in legislative bodies.[22] If they are able to assume this role, black legislators will increase their bargaining position within the governmental bodies that control the resources for supporting decent educational systems for blacks. Similarly, black legislators would also be in a position to press for other programs in housing, employment, health, welfare, and so forth. Such programs would improve the general quality of life in central cities and also, presumably, the out-of-school environment of future black students. This point is particularly important when one recalls that numerous studies show out-of-school environment to be a significant determinant of educational achievement.

In conclusion, the future of education in our large cities will hinge upon the outcome of several political struggles. At the local level, conflict will center on who controls the school system. At the state and federal levels, conflict will center on the ability of black legislators to gain bargaining power that will result in a greater allocation of fiscal resources to cities for support of educational and non-educational programs. Only if blacks are at least moderately successful in winning these battles will the quality of education in American cities be measurably improved.

Given the traditional image of school governance, many people may disagree with the suggestion that educational outcomes will be

---

[22] Recent events in the Illinois State Legislature provide an example of the possibilities along these lines. During the 1969 legislative session, a bipartisan bloc of black legislators successfully tied up proceedings over departmental budgets via a filabuster. Budgets were approved only after the blacks were successful in attaining a pledge that state departments would hire more blacks and money was allocated for on-the-job training programs.

largely determined by political factors. But the experience of the 1960's indicates that this is indeed the case. All major efforts to reform the public school system in the 1960's were constrained by political considerations, and were eventually decided politically. Such will certainly be the case during the 1970's. The immediate past has demonstrated that the quality of education available to groups in American society is not unrelated to the political power of the various groups. Leaders in the black community recognize this fact, and will therefore seek political power in the decade ahead as a means to upgrade the education provided for black students. The schools, far from being isolated in an apolitical atmosphere, will continue to be in the thick of intensive political conflicts as the black community attempts to achieve independence and to gain control of the institutions which shape the life-chances of black citizens. At this point, it is difficult to tell whether the black community will be successful or not; however, it is clear that the battle will be waged and that the future of urban education rests in the balance.

Index

Administrative reform, 148-149
AFL-CIO, 71, 109, 113
Allen, James E., 54
American Association of University Professors, 109
American Association of University Women, 109
American Federation of Teachers, 71, 72, 109
Americans for Democratic Action, 109
American Jewish Congress, 112
American Parents Committee, 109
American Veterans Committee, 109
Anti-poverty program, 74
Armstrong Act, 101
Atlanta, 2, 3

Bailey, Stephen K., 89, 95-96, 122
Baltimore, 13
Banfield, Edward, 4
Baptist, Joint Committee on Public Affairs, 112
Barden, Graham, 123
Bell, Wendell, 37
Benson, Charles C., 94
Berger, Bennett M., 35
Berkeley, California, 64
Bestor, Arthur E., 90
Birkhead, Guthrie, 38
Black control of schools, 155-158
Black, Justice Hugo, 111
Black power, 74, 155-156
Black schools:
  inferior conditions, 62
Black students:
  achievement levels, 60
  concentration in cities, 26-28
  dropout levels, 60
Board of education:
  election practices, 7-10
  function of, 6-7